The Best of
Silver Hills

Delicious Vegetarian Cuisine
Eileen and Debbie Brewer

Recipes on cover:
Fish Sticks --- page 64 with Tartar Sauce --- page 108
Potato Wedges --- page 85
Walnut Burger --- page 56
Potato Salad --- page 93

ISBN: 0-9681507-0-5

© **1996 by Eileen Brewer and Debbie Brewer**

Silver Hills Publishing
Lumby, British Columbia, Canada
Editor: Cathy Conroy
Design & Layout: Joel McComb
Photography: Free Spirit Studio
Illustrations: Joel McComb
Printing: Allegra Print and Imaging/Abbotsford

Printed in Canada at Allegra Print and Imaging, Abbotsford, British Columbia, Canada   Tel: 604-504-1677

**For a Distributor near you,
please call toll free 1-866-304-7060**

Acknowled ████████

To produce a successful publication requires more than just the words of the writers. A project like this requires the efforts of a team of talented people. To this end, the authors would like to gratefully acknowledge the contributions made by the following individuals:

Phil, husband, dad for sharing his knowledge on health and nutrition and for taking time from his busy schedule to write for our cookbook. **Catherine Conroy**, editor, for consulting and text editing. **Joel**, for his magic and artistry with the layout and graphics. **Free Spirit Studio (photography)**, much gratitude for making our recipes look as delicious as they taste. **John**, for answering our many questions and inspiring us in the culinary field. **Roxanne and Beverly**, for their artistic help and the many hours they put in preparing for the photography. Lori, for being a phone call away. And to all the folks at **Allegra Print and Imaging** for holding our hand through the maze of publishing.

The Staff at the Silver Hills Guest House, who helped us with everything from testing recipes to chopping vegetables.

The Bay, The Olive Bough, Kitchen It and many of our friends, who provided us with the dishes that so beautifully complimented our culinary creations.

And last, but not least, to all of the folks who have stayed with us at the Silver Hills Guest House and to all of our friends and family who have visited with us there over the years. These are the people who have provided us with their feedback, encouragement, recipes and cooking hints. Without them, none of this would have been possible.

God bless you all,

Eileen & Debbie

Table of Contents

Introduction

by Phil Brewer

Like most accomplishments, success does not occur overnight. *The Best of Silver Hills* cookbook actually began taking shape over 25 years ago. When Eileen and I met in 1971, it may have been a case of love at first sight, but it was definitely not a case of compatibility in the kitchen. Eileen was eating a traditional North American mixed diet of meat, chicken, eggs and dairy products while I was eating vegetarian meals occasionally supplemented with cheese, eggs, butter and meat analogs (prepared soy products). In a manner typical to true love, we each tried to convert to the other's lifestyle. I sampled some bacon and a few hamburgers, but soon discovered that I was not destined to be a meat eater. Likewise, Eileen tried eating my fake meat and found it equally hard to swallow. We finally compromised on a *lacto-ova* vegetarian diet, which included grains, fruits, vegetables and dairy products such as sour cream, cottage cheese, eggs and butter. With these foods Eileen could quickly and easily prepare delicious main meals and desserts that satisfied us both.

Our dietary compromise continued happily until our daughter Debbie was born lactose intolerant. Her condition meant that a large portion of our diet would create serious health problems for her. Eileen believed that she could simply eliminate the dairy products in her recipes and use sunflower oil instead. And so for the next while we ate sunflower oil in patties, cookies, sauces and desserts. Although these foods tasted similar, the exchange results were undesirable. Like other refined oils, sunflower oil is a highly processed food that lacks essential vitamins, minerals and fiber.

A year later, we eliminated the eggs, butter, cheeses and most of the polyunsaturated fats from our table and embarked on a total vegetarian or *vegan* diet. The results were dry—dry bread without butter, dry potatoes without gravy and dry desserts without sauces or toppings. Thus began Silver Hills' five lean years. In an effort to return some of the variety and excitement to our meals, Eileen began experimenting with various egg, sugar and butter substitutes in hundreds of recipes and then sampling the results. Bite by bite, she developed a collection of wonderful non-dairy, vegetarian recipes that we all could enjoy. Her new recipes produced foods that looked, smelled and tasted delicious. The results of Eileen and Debbie's hard work are contained here in *The Best of Silver Hills* cookbook and we hope you and your family will enjoy them too.

Vegetarian Kitchen Starter Kit

Here is a list of items that you may or may not have in your kitchen or on your shelves but will need to make the recipes in this cookbook as well as other vegetarian dishes. If you already have things like brown sugar, flour or seasonings that are similar, feel free to use whatever you have on hand. There is no need to go on a huge shopping trip before you have tried a few of the recipes and decided which of the foods you like best.

All of these items should be readily available in your local supermarket and/or health food store. If you have trouble locating these or other vegetarian food items not listed here, let us know. We may be able to help you find them or get them to you.

Try placing a check mark beside the items listed here that you already have. Then review the recipes you plan to make. Place an x beside the items you will need to get in order to prepare those dishes.

We recommend that you purchase a small amount of these missing ingredients to start. Once you've decided you like the recipes and want to continue cooking vegetarian, then consider buying in bulk.

Beans
Garbanzo beans
Kidney beans
Lentils
Navy beans
Pinto beans
Soy beans

Dried Fruits
Apricots
Cranberries
Dates
Papaya
Pineapple
Raisins

Flour & Grains
Bread yeast
Brown rice
Cornmeal
Gluten flour
Millet flour

Quick oats
Rye flour
Soy flour
Unbleached white flour
Wheat germ
Whole wheat flour

Nuts & Seeds
Almonds
Caraway seeds
Cashews (raw)
Coconut (unsweetened)
Flaxseed
Pecans
Sunflower seeds (unsalted)
Walnuts

Oils, Sugars & Flavorings
Brown sugar or

cane sugar substitute
Carob powder & chips
Honey (creamed or liquid)
Liquid lecithin
Maple flavoring
Maple syrup
Molasses
Olive oil
Vegetable oil spray
White vanilla

Pasta
Alphabets pasta
Fettuccine
Lasagna
Manicotti
Shell pasta
Spaghetti

Precooked, Canned or Commercial Products

All bran cereal

Bacon bits substitute such as *Baco*

Cornflakes

Garbanzo beans

Kidney beans

Maple syrup

Olives

Pickles

Pineapple juice

Salsa

Soy sauce (low salt)

Tomatoes

Tomato juice

Tomato paste

Vegetable oil spray

Seasonings & Baking Ingredients

Baking powder (health)

Beef-style seasoning

Cayenne

Chicken seasoning (vegetarian)

Cornstarch

Cumin

Dill

Egg replacement product such as *Egg Replacer*

Garlic powder

Gelatin powders, plain and flavored (*Emes* or other vegetable-based gelatin)

Cold liquid thickener such as *Cera Gel*

Italian seasoning

Minute tapioca

Nutritional yeast

Onion powder

Paprika

Parsley flakes

Sage

Sea salt

Herbamare or salt substitute

Spaghetti seasoning

Summer savory

Sweet basil

Tofu milk powder

Turmeric

Fresh Foods & Cooking Utensils

Following is a list of foods you will have to purchase fresh as you need them to make your recipes and meals:

Avocados

Fruits in season

Lemons for fresh lemon juice

Potatoes

Soy cheese

Tofu

Tofu milk

Vegetables in season

Here are just a few items that we have found to be invaluable in our kitchen:

Blender

Cookie sheets (2 or 3 non-stick variety)

Food Processor

Hand grater

Hot air corn popper

Ice cream scoops (various sizes)

Juicer (optional)

Knives (a good set of sharp, stainless steel)

Kitchen scraper (hard edged plastic for removing dough from bowls and countertops)

Loaf pans (3 or 4)

Plastic storage containers & lids (various sizes suitable for freezer)

Wok or thick bottomed pan

Non-stick frying pan

Meal & Menu Planning

Most of the homemakers and professional cooks we have spoken with agree that taking the time to plan meals in advance takes much of the frustration and anxiety out of food preparation.

The key to successful vegetarian cooking is to plan a weekly or bi-weekly menu that includes a wide variety of fruits, nuts, grains and vegetables. It also helps to plan your menus around fresh fruits and vegetables as they come into season. Not only are they tastier at that time, they are also less expensive.

A menu planner also helps with the weekly grocery shopping. With a meal plan, you know exactly what you need to get so that you aren't running to the store at the last minute to pick up that forgotten item. It also ensures that you purchase only what you need and that unused fruits or vegetables don't waste away in the fridge. A menu plan doesn't mean you can't change your mind about what to make and when, but it does give you a solid platform from which to start.

When menu planning, you should also take into consideration the foods that you and your family like to eat as well as the foods that are good for you. It is important that you not only get the nutritional value from your meals, but also that mealtimes are a relaxing and enjoyable part of the day.

You may want to consider planning daily meals around certain grains and vegetables. For instance, Mondays might be 'bean' day, and Monday's main meal will feature a certain type or variety of bean. Tuesdays might be 'rice' day, Wednesdays 'tofu' day and so on.

At Silver Hills, our daily menus are based on the premise that a substantial breakfast, a complete or main-meal lunch and a light supper is the healthiest and most efficient way for the body to process food. We also plan our daily meals so that we allow sufficient time for the stomach to digest one meal before we give it another. To this end, we allow approximately 5 to 6 hours between meals. We realize that, for various reasons, not everyone will be able to follow this type of meal schedule.

To help you with the menu planning process, we have provided you with a sample Two-week Menu Planner (see foldout at the back of the book). You might want to try following our menus for one or two days to see how you like them. Feel free to add and substitute recipes and entrées to suit your family's tastes.

The trick to successful menu planning is to be organized and to think ahead. If you examine the sample Two-week Menu Planner you will see how the menus have been organized to save work and time. For example:

• On Sunday, Week #1, cook enough rice for Sunday's Walnut Rice Loaf (see page 54), Monday's Fried Rice (see page 71) and Wednesday's Walnut Burgers (see page 56). Cooked rice will keep several days in the fridge and you won't have to start your rice-based dishes from scratch each time.

• On Friday, Week #2, cook enough Tomato Pasta Sauce (see page 77) for Friday's French Bread Pizza (see page 119) as well as Saturday's Tofu Manicotti (see page 78).

• On Wednesday, Week #1, peel enough potatoes to make Potato Wedges (see page 85). Then peel and cook the extra potatoes you will need to make Tillie's Potatoes (see page 85) on Saturday. Cooked potatoes will also keep several days in the fridge.

Our menu plans also take into consideration the problem of 'leftovers'. In fact, leftovers often become the basis for other meals. For example:

• Serve the leftover gravy from Tuesday's (Week #2) Irish Stew (see page 68) with Ingrid's Walnut Balls (see page 65) on Thursday.

Many of our entree dishes freeze quite nicely. So, if you have the space in your freezer, you will save time by doubling the recipes you like as you make them. For instance, make a double recipe of Fish Sticks (see page 64), cook the ones you need for dinner and freeze the rest for another meal. Freeze your foods in meal-sized packages. That way you won't be thawing a huge package of beans or cooked rice or fresh peas when all you need is a couple of cups.

If possible, try to make up all your basics—the milks, jams, butters and cheeses—all in one day or evening so that you will have enough to last you the week.

Finally, plan your meals to suit your family's food needs. People who work hard physically often require a heartier meal than those who spend most of their day behind a desk. If you find that you constantly have leftover entrees, vegetables and desserts in your fridge, cut back on the quantity you make. Also, take climate and temperature into consideration when menu planning; they often play a large part in determining the type and amount of food you elect to serve.

Review the fold-out Two-week Menu Planner. Try as many of the selections as you like. The titles that are bolded indicate that the recipe for that dish is in this cookbook. We've also provided you with a blank Two-week Menu Planner for you to practice menu planning. Make copies and get the kids to help you fill it in. When you plan ahead, meal preparation can be a fun and enjoyable part of your daily routine.

Cooking Suggestions

This section contains some basic suggestions, tips and hints on how to assemble and prepare ingredients for vegetarian recipes. Although this section has been written with vegetarian cooking in mind, many of the suggestions provided here also apply to more traditional cooking. You may want to review this section before you begin preparing your meals.

Roasts & Patties

• Most roasts and patties consist of a nut, a grain, a binder and seasonings. Don't be afraid to add a little more rice or bread crumbs to roast/loaf mixtures that appear too moist. If you find that they are too dry, increase the amount of liquid or cream. You want your roasts and loafs to have a nice firm consistency when they come out of the oven.

• When you're making rice-based patties, you'll need a slightly moister mixture so that the patties will stick together as you form them and not fall apart during cooking. Add your liquids a little at a time until you achieve the desired consistency. A tablespoon or two of garbanzo flour also acts as a good binding agent.

• Most of our patties and roasts freeze quite nicely. To save time, make an extra loaf or another batch of patties and freeze them for another day. Try not to cook the same thing over and over again. Variety is one of the keys to enjoyable eating.

Beans

• Prepare beans by first letting them soak overnight. Then drain and rinse them in cold water. Place the rinsed beans in a pot with just enough cold water to cover them. Cover the pot, bring them to a boil and drain again. Again, pour in enough cold water to cover. Cover the pot, and again, bring to a boil. Then reduce the heat and let them simmer until cooked. Once the beans are cooked they can be used immediately or frozen in small packages ready for your favorite recipes.

The following chart indicates the approximate cooking times for different types of beans:

Bean Type	Cooking time
garbanzoes	4 to 6 hours
green split peas	45 to 60 minutes
kidney beans	2 to 3 hours
lentils	45 to 60 minutes
navy beans	2 to 3 hours
pinto beans	2 to 3 hours
soy beans	4 to 6 hours

Tofu

• Tofu is a soybean product that comes in either soft, medium, firm or dessert form. Most of our recipes call for medium tofu; however, feel free to use whichever type you prefer. Grocery stores now carry a number of different brands of tofu and each brand seems to have a slightly different taste. We suggest that you experiment with a few to see which ones you like best.

• After opening the package, rinse the tofu in cold water and allow it to drain. Use a paper towel to absorb the excess moisture. Place your unused tofu in a container, cover it with water and seal tightly. It will keep in the fridge for about a week. However, to keep the stored tofu fresh, you must remember to rinse it and replace the water in the container every day.

• Tofu is usually prepared and served in one of three ways:

- Cubed and cooked in recipes such as stir fry vegetables.

- Blended and cooked in patties, rice loaves and desserts.

- Crumbled and cooked in recipes such as scrambled eggs, manicotti filling, egg rolls, lasagna filling, cottage cheese and fish stick batter.

Grains

• Basically, all grains are cooked in the same manner. The only difference is in the cooking time and the amount of water added. Place your measured grain in boiling water and add salt to taste. Cover the pot and reduce the heat to simmer.

The following chart indicates the approximate cooking times for different types of grains:

Grain	Amount	Water	Cooking Time
quick oats	1 cup	2 cups	5 minutes
large flake oats	1 cup	2 cups	30 minutes
whole oats	3/4 cup	2 cups	1 to 2 hours
pearl barley	1 cup	2 cups	45 minutes
oat bran	2/3 cup	2 cups	5 minutes
rice	1 cup	2 cups	1 hour
millet	1 cup	3 cups	1 hour
seven grain	1 cup	3 cups	1 hour
cornmeal	1 cup	4 cups	30 minutes

• When cooking brown rice, the standard formula is one part rice to two parts water. A heavy pot, with a snug lid, seems to cook rice better than a lighter pot. Start with boiling water. Then add the rice, cover and let it cook over a low heat for about an hour. You can also use the same process and bake your rice in a tightly covered casserole dish in the oven. Like beans, cooked rice can be used right away or placed in meal-sized packages and kept in the freezer until you need them.

• A crock pot is a convenient way to cook any of the above combination of grains. Here's an easy way to make a hot Three Grain Cereal for breakfast: Before you go to bed, put 1/3 cup wheat, 1/3 cup oats and 1/3 cup barley (or any other combination of three grains) into your crock pot. Add 2 1/2 to 3 cups water and salt to taste. Plug the crock pot in, turn it to low and let it cook all night. In the morning, your hot cereal will be ready and waiting for you.

Pasta

• Cook pasta according to the directions on the pasta package. If you find you have more cooked pasta than your recipe calls for here are a few things you can do with those leftovers:

- Make a basic cream sauce and season it with chicken style seasoning, onion powder and celery salt. Pour it over the bowl of cooked pasta. Stir in a few sautéed onion and celery pieces, green peppers and/or other vegetables. Bake the whole works up in an attractive casserole dish and serve. Makes a great one-dish meal.

- Put leftover pasta in a frying pan. Sprinkle with chicken style seasoning and onion powder and fry until the pasta turns crispy and golden brown. Makes a quick and tasty side dish.

- Use it in your favorite chicken or other noodle soup recipes.

Fresh or Canned Fruit

• We are fortunate to be living in a time when a variety of fresh and canned fruit is almost always readily available. However, do try to eat fresh fruits as they come into season. They are usually tastier and less expensive. If possible, try and take advantage of the seasonal abundance to freeze or can your favorite fruits so that you can enjoy them throughout the year. Try to select the best grade of fruit; we've found it's better to purchase and enjoy a few large, sweet and juicy pears or peaches than to have throw out a dozen small sour ones.

• Wash and then serve fresh fruit slightly chilled or just below room temperature. Store fruit in a crisper or cool portion of the fridge.

• You can sweeten fruit a number of different ways. A little apple juice concentrate or pineapple juice or grape juice make excellent natural sweeteners. You can also add a little honey or sugar to water (1 part sweetening to 6 parts water) to make a light syrup for your fruit.

• Making your own fruit fillings for pies and tarts is less expensive and healthier than buying the canned pie fillings; and everyone loves a homemade fruit pie.

Vegetables

• Fresh vegetables are one of the staples of the vegetarian diet. But even they need to be cooked and served in ways that are attractive and appealing.

To perk up steamed cauliflower, try pan frying a few shredded carrots until they turn bright orange. Then place them around your mound of cauliflower pieces. Sprinkle the works with a bit of fresh parsley and you have a very attractive serving of vegetables.

To liven up a dish of peas, cut a few strips of carrots into thin, 1- to 2-inch pieces; then cook and serve the two together.

Drizzling a little melted Jack Cheese (see page 100) over steamed broccoli flowers or asparagus spears makes them look really tasty.

• Never overcook fresh vegetables! Overcooking reduces their flavor and gives them a limp, worn out appearance.

Salads & Salad Plates

• A fresh salad is not only nutritious, it also gives your meal that "alive" appearance and sets off the other items on your menu.

• When preparing any salad or salad plate, use only quality vegetables. Rinse them in cold water and drain or spin to remove the excess water. Include a variety of green and red vegetables in all your salads. Remember, color and texture are the basis of an appealing dish. Top the salads with sprigs of parsley or any of your favorite garnishes.

• Crispen up any wilted greens (lettuce, spinach, celery and so on) by soaking them in cold water for 15 to 20 minutes before you add them to the salad bowl.

• The menu's main dish usually determines if a tossed salad or a salad plate should be served with that meal. For example, when you're serving burgers or other patties, prepare a salad plate of sliced fresh vegetables such as tomatoes, green peppers, cucumbers and so on. Sprouts, tomatoes, onions and avocado slices make a nice salad plate to serve with sandwiches.

A stir-fry vegetable entree is already full of vegetables so you don't really need a tossed salad to accompany it. Instead, prepare a side salad plate of carrot sticks, peppers and olives.

A tossed salad goes nicely with a roast/loaf or pasta entree. Make sure to serve a couple of different salad dressings with the tossed salad.

• For a quick and easy salad, place a few crisp carrot sticks, sliced peppers, cucumber spears, tomato wedges and green onions on two or three leaves of fresh lettuce. Serve with your favorite salad dressing or veggie dip.

Seasonings

• Whenever you are adding seasonings or flavorings, remember that different brands of seasoning will each have a slightly different taste and some will be stronger than others. Get to know the seasonings on your shelf.

• Every so often, check your seasonings to make sure they are still fresh. Although dried seasonings will last a long time, the older they get, the less flavor they have. If you add a teaspoon of sage to a recipe and find that there is little or no sage flavor, it's probably time to replace that seasoning.

• Use seasonings sparingly—you can always add more if you like, but it's difficult to remove a flavor once it's in the pot.

• If the recipe calls for a seasoning that you don't like, feel free to substitute it for one that you prefer.

• To produce a beefy flavor, use soy sauce, *Maggi*, beef style seasoning, yeast extract and/or nutritional yeast as your seasonings. For a chicken or fish flavor, add chicken style seasoning, nutritional yeast, sage and/or celery salt.

Desserts

• Because our pie crusts are made without butter or lard, we add yeast to give them a lighter, flakier appearance and texture. However, the lack of fat means that our crusts bake in about half the amount of time a regular pie crust requires. To avoid having burnt crusts and cooked fruit or baked crusts and raw fruit, you must precook your raw fruit fillings (apples, cherries, peaches, etc.) before you bake them in these pie crusts.

• Many of our cake and cookie recipes follow the same basic formula: Blend cashews and water, honey or cane sugar substitute and *Egg Replacer* or Flaxseed Gel (see page 111). Add flour, baking powder and flavorings and bake. However, from there you can let your imagination take over. Try using different sizes and shapes of cake or baking pans. Add raisins, currents or other dried fruits to the batter. Before baking, sprinkle with a dusting of nuts or icing sugar or dot with fanned, fresh apple slices or glazed fruit pieces. It's often the finishing touches that make the dessert a special treat.

• Make an icing from melted carob chips and spread it over the cooled cake. Put 1 cup of carob chips in a bowl and heat for 1 minute in the microwave. If they have not melted enough to stir, microwave for another 20 seconds and check again. Don't begin to stir the carob until it is completely melted or it will turn hard.

Meals

• Our breakfasts generally include a hot cereal, a "special" and a granola. However, your family may not need or want that much food every morning. Assemble your breakfast foods to suit your family's needs and tastes. For many, a serving of granola, toast and fruit or just toast and fruit will be sufficient. Decide what it is you like and work from there. We have no hard and fast rules about what should be served. It is more important that you enjoy a good, nutritious breakfast.

• One of the most neglected aspects of many meals is its appearance. When you present foods that look attractive, people are more likely to enjoy them, and even digest them better. When preparing your dishes, try to visualize how the foods are going to look on your table.

To enhance food appearance, think in terms of color, texture and variety. For instance, placing a few sprigs of parsley on sautéed carrots or steamed cauliflower adds color and interest to a plain dish of vegetables. A sprig of mint on a lemon sauce or a dash of cinnamon on a vanilla pudding perks up an everyday dessert. Use your imagination, but don't go overboard. Remember, when decorating foods, less is often more.

Kitchen Equipment

• To prepare good foods you need dependable, but not necessarily expensive, kitchen equipment. However, if you do decide to purchase a new kitchen appliance or utensil, we have found that quality does make a difference.

• For vegetarian cooking, a **blender** is essential. It is probably the only electrical appliance you really do need. There are all types and varieties of blenders on the market today. Shop around until you find one that suits your needs and budget.

• A **juicer** is a "nice to have" appliance. The *Champion Juicer* for instance does three different jobs. In addition to juicing, it makes great peanut and nut butters as well as frozen ice creams. If you watch your newspaper, you might be able to pick up a second-hand one for a reasonable amount.

• A **slow cooker** or **crock pot,** although not essential, can come in handy for cooking grains and cereals and for cooking or heating up items that tend to burn such as gravies, soups and sauces. They also make cooking beans, soups and stews something you can do when you're not at home.

• **Microwave ovens** are great for quick cooking, sautéing or steaming fresh vegetables, melting carob chips and reheating leftovers.

• A **hot air corn popper** is a handy way to prepare Popcorn (see page 120), which we often serve as a snack or as a side dish with our light suppers.

• A **rice cooker** is a great, quick way to prepare rice.

• A **set of good cooking utensils** including spatulas, scrapers, knives, peelers and so on is essential. Things like good cutting boards, food storage containers and non-stick baking dishes and fry pans tend to make cooking quicker, easier and less frustrating.

More cooking tips and hints are included in the recipe sections of this cookbook. Look for the **TIP** icon beside the recipes.

Our best suggestion for cooking any meal is to prepare and serve the foods you enjoy in a manner that will appeal to the eye as well as the taste buds.

Blending Tips

Because many of the recipes in this cookbook require the ingredients to be blended, we have included a few tips on how to make sure your blended mixtures turn out right.

In vegetarian food preparation, correct blending procedures are essential. In fact, it is the step that often determines the success of the recipe. Whenever the recipe direction reads "Blend until smooth and creamy", it means exactly that.

To blend completely smooth often requires some time. Put your cashews and water in the blender, turn it on and let it run for at least 3 to 4 minutes. While it is blending you can rinse a few dishes or prepare the ingredients for the next step in the recipe. It's so important to blend the basics to a smooth, creamy consistency, particularly in sauces, butters, ice creams and gravies. Your basic mixture should be completely smooth and have no visible gritty particles. If necessary, rub a little of the mixture between your fingers. If it still feels gritty, it needs more blending.

When blending nuts to form a cream, add only enough water to the blender so that the nuts don't become stuck or your blender begins to labor. Try adding a few tablespoons of liquid at a time until you achieve the desired consistency. If that means adding more liquid than the recipe calls for, do so.

Some nuts are harder to blend than others. For instance, cashews and walnuts are the easiest to blend. Almonds are drier and will require a little more water and blending time to reach a creamy texture. If necessary, you can substitute blanched almonds for raw cashews, but they will take longer to blend smooth.

Always make sure that you have added enough liquid or mixture so that the blender blades are completely submerged. If they aren't, the items simply won't cream. If the mixture level appears too low, just add enough water to cover the blades.

If you need to blend coconut into a cream, first blend it by itself in a dry blender until it reaches a smooth, almost liquid consistency. Then add the liquid.

When making bread crumbs or grinding nuts or coarse flours, you must have a completely dry blender jar. So blend up these items first. Even though your blender may look dry after you have rinsed and wiped it out, chances are it will still be damp inside. Blending dry ingredients in a damp blender will simply produce mush.

Read through the recipe before you begin. Add the bulkier items to the blender last. That way you will ensure that the nuts are blended well and your seasonings are thoroughly mixed. For example, in Tofu Mayonnaise (see page 96), tofu is the last ingredient to be added to the blender; in Corn Butter (see page 109), the cooked cereal goes in last.

It's inconvenient to be constantly washing out your blender each time you use it. Therefore, try to do most of your blending at one time. That way you only have to rinse out the blender jar after each blend. Then you can keep right on going.

As always, our best advice is to read each recipe thoroughly before you begin. You may even want to do a few taste tests as you add seasonings or flavorings to the blended mixtures. Remember, you can always add more of something, but you can't take it out once it's in the blender.

Breads

Breads

by Phil Brewer

Early in our marriage, Eileen and I made our first attempt at changing and improving our lifestyle. In an effort to "eat healthier", we made a New Year's resolution not to buy any more "store-made" breads; from here on in, we would bake our own bread. How difficult could this be? With the spirit of resolution burning, Eileen purchased 20 pounds of enriched white flour, yeast and a couple of bread pans. Our bakery opened early the next morning with Eileen kneading dough and forming loaves. Together, we appreciated the wonderful aroma of our healthy bread baking in our own oven and eagerly anticipated the tasty outcome.

Unfortunately, the results were somewhat less than we expected. Our healthy loaves of bread just weren't that big, in fact these loaves were downright puny. However, it was taste that mattered. As soon as they cooled, I cut a slice from one of the loaves. Where I had been expecting a light, tasty homemade texture and flavor, I saw a sticky, doughy mess. This bread wasn't even edible. I was on my way out to the grocery store.

Eileen however was undaunted. She possesses that one important quality that is essential to any successful lifestyle change. She refused to give up at the first failed attempt; our goal to healthier living would not be hindered by a couple of bad loaves of bread. She dumped the first batch into the garbage and started over. An hour later the smell of baking bread was again wafting through our kitchen, and lo, another batch of uncooked, doughy bread lumps. Something was definitely not working.

At this point I decided it must be the cook who was doing something wrong. Once I took over the operation things would be different. And six hours from the time we opened our bakery that morning, we were blessed with our third batch of inedible bread. We agreed that it was the bad bag of flour that was causing the problems.

After some reading and research, we purchased a small amount of flour and followed the directions given. Not leaving anything to chance, we even said a small prayer before we began. The result—a resounding success. Homemade bread had never tasted so good. We didn't even need our New Year's resolution to keep us going; after all we'd been through we couldn't possibly eat store-bought bread again.

Obviously, the moral of this story has more to do with making a resolve to change to a healthier way of living than it has to do with making bread. For any lifestyle change to be effective and lasting requires more than just a desire to change. You must also have the right set of tools and the correct information to help you to keep that resolve in place. As you consider moving to a new way of cooking, eating and living, examine the alternatives, ask questions, experiment and finally, don't be afraid to fail. It is the failures that make us truly appreciate life's successes. Like our home-made bread, the final results will be extremely satisfying.

Nutritionists have been working hard to fracture North Americans' love affair with white bread and white flour products. Even the "enriched" white breads are poor substitutes for whole grain loaves. Enriched flour lacks the bran or outer protective coating of the grain's kernel. Bran is the indigestible fiber that absorbs water in the digestive tract. It helps to provide bulk and stimulate the normal movements of the bowel. According to many doctors, it is the lack of these indigestible fibers in our diet that promote conditions such as constipation and other digestive tract diseases including colon cancer.

Therefore, the next time you go out to buy your bread and bread products, avoid the white bread. Look for items that are made from whole grains or with whole wheat flour. Most grocery stores carry an excellent selection of these healthier alternatives. They're just as tasty and your digestive system will thank you.

Basic Bread or Bun Dough

4	cups	very warm water
¼	cup	brown sugar or a cane sugar substitute
2	cups	rolled oats
1½	tbsp	salt
2	tbsp	yeast
2	tbsp	gluten flour (optional)
2	tbsp	liquid lecithin
8	cups	flour (whole wheat and unbleached white)

1. Mix all of the above ingredients **except the flour** in a large mixing bowl or bread mixer.
2. Add 3 cups flour. Let stand for 5 minutes.
3. Continue to add remaining flour until you have a soft, kneadable dough that no longer sticks to the side of the bowl. Knead for 10 minutes.
4. Let dough rise for 20 minutes in a warm place.
5. Preheat oven to 350°. Divide and shape dough into loaves or buns. Place in oiled pans and let rise 30 minutes.
6. Bake for 45 minutes.
7. Turn out of pans and allow bread to cool before serving. For variety, try adding 1 cup of raisins or nuts to the dough before you add the bulk of the flour.

Makes 4 medium loaves or 3 dozen buns

You can choose how light or heavy you want your bread to be by varying the amount of whole wheat and unbleached white flour you use.

Make the entire Basic Bread recipe. Use half the dough to make 2 bread loaves and use the rest to make a dozen buns or a tea ring or a maple nut twist or a dozen sweet rolls.

Sweet Rolls

1. Make only half of the Basic Bread recipe or use half of the dough from the whole Basic Bread recipe. Follow the recipe instructions up to and including step 4.
2. After the dough has risen, divide the mixture in half. Place one half on a floured counter top and roll it out to form a rectangle about ¼" thick.
3. Spread Corn Butter (see page 109) on the flattened dough. Then sprinkle evenly with brown sugar or cane sugar substitute, cinnamon, nuts and raisins. Beginning at one edge, roll dough up to form a log.
4. Cut the log into sections, each about 3" long. Place these sections, cut side down and about 2" apart, onto a vegetable oil-sprayed cookie sheet. Let rise 10 minutes.
5. Bake at 350° for 45 minutes. Allow rolls to cool before serving.

Makes 15 Sweet Rolls

TP

To make sweet rolls that stay soft, bake them in an oiled glass casserole dish with a little maple syrup dribbled on the bottom.

Tea Ring

1. Make only half of the Basic Bread recipe or use half of the dough from the whole Basic Bread recipe. Follow the recipe instructions up to and including step 4.
2. After the dough has risen, place it on a floured counter top and roll it out to form a rectangle about ¼" thick.
3. Spread flattened dough with your favorite fruit mixture such as cherry filling or apple filling. Sprinkle nuts, cinnamon, and brown sugar evenly over spread fruit.
4. Beginning at one edge, roll dough up to form a long log. Carefully lift and place the log on a vegetable oil-sprayed cookie sheet. Make sure the seam is on the bottom. Join the ends of the log together to form a ring.
5. Make ¼" slits every 4 or 5 inches along the top of roll so that it fans out as it bakes.
6. Bake in preheated oven set at 350° for 45 minutes.
7. After cooling, drizzle a little icing along the top and decorate with nuts or candied fruit. Cut and serve.

Serves 8

Step 5

Maple Nut Twist

1. Make only half of the Basic Bread recipe
   (see page 22). Follow the recipe instructions up to and including step 4.
2. In a small bowl, mix together 1½ cups
   brown sugar or a cane sugar substitute, 1
   cup finely chopped walnuts and 1 teaspoon maple flavoring.
3. Divide the bread dough into thirds, each
   third about the size of a tennis ball. On a
   floured counter top, roll out each ball to
   form a round, ¼" thick dough circle that
   will fit into a medium-sized pizza pan.
4. Place the first dough circle on the bottom
   of a vegetable oil-sprayed pizza pan.
   Spread evenly with Corn Butter (see page
   109) or butter substitute of your choice.
   Sprinkle one third of the brown sugar
   mixture over the buttered dough.
5. Place the second dough circle on top of
   first. Butter it and sprinkle with another
   third of brown sugar mixture. Repeat this
   process with the last dough circle.
6. Place a medium-sized drinking glass or
   cup in the center of the pizza pan. Using a
   sharp knife, cut spokes in the dough layers from the lip of the cup out to edge of
   the pan. Cut 16 spokes evenly around the
   glass.
7. Twist each of the 16 dough pieces 5 times.
   Let rise 10 minutes.
8. Bake in a preheated oven at 350° for
   about 30 minutes or until golden brown.
9. Serve warm as part of a dessert tray or
   with fresh fruit.

Makes 17 servings

Step 6

Step 7

Banana Bread

1	cup	mashed ripe bananas
⅔	cup	brown sugar or cane sugar substitute
¼	cup	olive oil or ¼ cup raw cashews blended smooth in ¼ cup water
½	cup	tofu milk
1	tbsp	lemon juice
1	tsp	cinnamon
½	cup	chopped walnuts or pecans
1	tbsp	*Egg Replacer* or other commercial egg replacement
½	tsp	salt
1 ½	cups	unbleached white flour
3	tsp	baking powder

Makes 1 loaf

1. Preheat oven to 350°.
2. In a large bowl, mix all ingredients together until well combined.
3. Pour bread mixture into a loaf pan that has been well sprayed with oil. Bake for 45 minutes.
4. Turn out of pan and cool. Slice and serve with Corn Butter (see page 109) or jam.

Bran Muffins

1 ½	cups	commercial *All–Bran* cereal
1 ¼	cups	tofu milk
½	cup	brown sugar or cane sugar substitute
1	tbsp	*Egg Replacer* or other commercial egg replacement
½	cup	raisins
⅓	cup	molasses
1 ¼	cups	unbleached white flour
2	tsp	baking powder
¼	tsp	salt

Yields 12 muffins

TP

Use an ice cream scoop to spoon muffin batter into muffin tins.

1. Preheat oven to 375°.
2. In a large bowl combine bran cereal and tofu milk. Let stand for 5 minutes.
3. Add remaining ingredients and mix gently.
4. Spoon mixture into muffin tins that have been well sprayed with vegetable oil. Bake for 25 minutes.
5. Serve warm with jam.

Blueberry Muffins

1	cup	raw cashews
1	cup	water
½	cup	honey
½	tsp	salt
1	tsp	vanilla
1	tbsp	*Egg Replacer* or other commercial egg replacement
1	tsp	lemon juice
1 ¼	cups	unbleached white flour
2 ½	tsp	baking powder
2	cups	fresh or frozen, unsweetened blueberries

1. Preheat oven to 350°.
2. Place cashews and water into blender and blend until very smooth.
3. Add remaining ingredients **except flour, baking powder and blueberries** to blender and continue blending until well combined.
4. Pour blended mixture into a large bowl. Add flour and baking powder and mix.
5. Stir in blueberries.
6. Spoon mixture into muffin tins that have been well sprayed with vegetable oil. Bake for 20 to 25 minutes.

Makes 12 muffins

 TIP

When using frozen fruit in muffins, add ¼ cup more flour.

 TIP

To make cranberry muffins, simply replace blueberries with 2 cups dried cranberries.

Corn Bread

1 ½	cups	corn meal
2 ½	cups	tofu milk
2	cups	unbleached white flour
1	tsp	salt
2	tsp	baking powder
¼	cup	honey
¼	cup	ground flax seed (optional)
¼	cup	olive oil

1. Preheat oven to 375°.
2. Mix milk and cornmeal together in a large bowl. Let stand 5 minutes.
3. Add remaining ingredients and mix well.
4. Pour mixture into an 8" x 12" pan that has been sprayed with oil.
5. Bake for 45 minutes or until inserted toothpick comes out clean.

Serves 6

 TIP

Add ½ cup shredded soy cheese or 1 tsp diced fresh jalapeno for a zestier corn bread flavor.

Rye Bread

2	cups	boiling water
½	cup	molasses
1 ½	tsp	salt
¼	cup	caraway seeds (optional)
2	tbsp	honey
1	cup	rye flour
½	cup	warm water
1	tbsp	yeast
1 ½	tsp	brown sugar or cane sugar substitute
2	cups	whole wheat flour
4	cups	unbleached white flour

1. Mix first six ingredients together in a large bowl and let cool until molasses mixture is just warm.
2. Dissolve yeast and brown sugar in ½ cup warm water and add to molasses mixture.
3. Stir in unbleached white flour and whole wheat flour until dough is soft enough to knead. Knead briskly 5 to 10 minutes.
4. Let rise approximately 30 minutes and then divide mixture into 2 round loaves.
5. Place both loaves on a vegetable oil-sprayed cookie sheet and let rise 20 minutes.
6. Bake for 1 hour in a preheated oven at 375°.
7. Allow bread to cool before slicing. Serve warm with jam or marmalade.

Goes nicely with baked brown beans or stew. Makes 2 medium-sized round loaves.

TIP

On a hot day, try giving the kids a slice of rye bread topped with cottage cheese, tomatoes, cucumbers and olives.

Italian Bread Sticks

2	cups	very warm water
¼	cup	brown sugar
2	tbsp	yeast
2	tsp	salt
¼	cup	olive oil
2	tbsp	Italian seasoning or spaghetti seasoning
½	tsp	garlic powder (optional)
½	tsp	onion powder (optional)
1	cup	whole wheat flour
4	cups	unbleached white flour

1. Mix all ingredients together and knead dough for 5 minutes. Let rise 20 minutes.
2. Preheat oven to 350°. Divide dough in half. Place one half on a floured counter top and roll it out to form a rectangle about ½" thick.
3. Place dough sheets on a vegetable oil-sprayed cookie sheet. Cut dough into thin strips about ½" apart along the width of the pan. Repeat this process with the remaining dough portion.
4. Bake for 30 minutes.
5. Serve warm with salads and entrees.

Makes about 12 bread sticks

TP

To make a great pizza crust, simply omit the Italian seasoning, garlic and onion powder from this recipe and roll to fit 2 medium sized pizza pans.

Cheese Biscuits

2	cups	unbleached white flour
1	cup	whole wheat flour
2	tsp	baking powder
1	tsp	salt
½	cup	shredded soy cheese
1½	cups	cold water
2	tbsp	olive oil

Serves 6

1. Preheat oven to 350°.
2. Place first five ingredients in a large bowl. Mix water and oil together and add to dry ingredients.
3. Stir only until soft dough forms.
4. Place dough on a floured surface and gently roll until it is about a ½" thick.
5. Cut into biscuit shapes, place on an oiled cookie sheet and bake for 30 minutes.

Breakfasts

Breakfasts

by Phil Brewer

These days, preventative medicine and holistic health are common topics of discussion. Invariably, the health guests who arrive at Silver Hills are familiar with terms such as blood cholesterol, anti-oxidants and body fat. Although most are extremely knowledgeable about such matters, the majority do not follow a planned, well structured health program, which includes developing and maintaining proper eating habits.

Establishing a good, sensible eating schedule is essential to healthy digestion. The common eating pattern of many North Americans involves downing a couple of cups of coffee for breakfast, grabbing a jellyroll at coffee break, eating a ham sandwich on white with a soft drink for lunch, snacking on junk foods in the afternoon, and finally, when the body's resources are at their lowest ebb, ingesting a huge dinner after work. It is this kind of eating pattern that eventually puts them in the hospital. As one health lecturer put it, "We often plan the disease we're going to die with."

When you hop out of bed in the morning, your digestive organs are at their peak, and your body's demand for energy is at its highest. Your body burns calories faster an hour after you wake up than it does at any other time of the day, which makes morning the best time to eat. For people who are concerned with weight gain, breakfast should be one of the larger meals of the day. A six-year army research project compared a group of soldiers who ate a 2,000 calorie breakfast with soldiers who ate a 2,000 calorie dinner. They discovered that the soldiers who ate the high-calorie breakfast all lost weight while the other group either gained or maintained weight. Another report describes how one man lost nearly 50 pounds by simply reversing the order of his daily meals.

Eating a breakfast high in complex carbohydrates reduces the urge to snack or nibble throughout the morning. A breakfast that includes whole grain breads, cereals and/or granolas causes the body to release energy slowly and helps to eliminate the mid-morning "sugar blues." On the other hand, a breakfast comprised of coffee, sugars and refined grains produces a quick energy release, and you spend the rest of the morning snacking in an effort to re-establish

the energy level your body needs to function.

Snacking and eating between meals lays the foundation for digestive weakness and breakdown. It has been demonstrated that simply having a banana between breakfast and lunch slows down the digestion of the breakfast foods. Even nibbling peanuts between meals triples the time it takes the body to digest its previous meal. Even eating the best low-fat, cholesterol-free foods randomly throughout the day is not as an effective way of maintaining health and controlling weight gain as simply eating a good breakfast, a healthy lunch and a light dinner.

Baked Leftover Cereal

1	cup	cooked oatmeal
1	cup	leftover cooked cereal
½	cup	raisins or dates
½	cup	raw cashews
1	cup	or enough water to blend
1	tbsp	honey
1	tsp	vanilla

1. In a bowl, mix together oatmeal, leftover cooked cereal and raisins or dates.
2. Blend cashews, water, honey and vanilla until very smooth.
3. Add blended mixture to your cereal combination and mix well.
4. Pour into a vegetable oil-sprayed, 8" square pan and bake at 350° for 30 to 40 minutes.
5. Serve with milk and fruit.

When we say leftover cereal, we literally mean just that. Use whatever cooked cereals you have left over such as seven grain, sunny boy, cornmeal mush, etc. to make this recipe.

Oat Waffles

4	cups	rolled oats
½	cup	ground millet or cornmeal
1	tsp	salt
1	tsp	vanilla
1	tbsp	maple flavoring
½	cup	almonds
5	cups	water

1. Mix all of the above ingredients in a large bowl, cover and let batter stand in the fridge for several hours or overnight.
2. When ready to cook, pour 2 cups of batter at a time into blender and blend until smooth. If necessary, add more water to achieve a pouring consistency.
3. Preheat waffle iron. Pour ½ to 1 cup (depending on the size of your waffle iron) of batter onto hot waffle iron and bake 10 to 12 minutes or until golden brown. Repeat procedure until batter is used.
4. Serve immediately with Corn Butter (see page 109) and your favorite jams or syrups.

Yields 6 to 8 waffles. Cooked waffles can be frozen.

TIP

To season a waffle iron: Heat the iron, then unplug and brush surface with vegetable shortening. Cool and wipe off excess with a paper towel. Plug in and reheat the iron. It is now ready for the batter.

Favorite Granola

8	cups	rolled oats
1	cup	coconut
1	cup	raw, unsalted sunflower seeds
1	cup	raw pumpkin seeds (optional)
1	cup	almonds
1	cup	maple syrup
1	tsp	salt
2	tbsp	vanilla
1	tbsp	maple flavoring

Makes approximately 12 cups

1. Preheat oven to 250°.
2. Mix all dry ingredients together in a large bowl.
3. Combine vanilla and maple flavoring with maple syrup. Add liquid to dry ingredients and mix well together.
4. Place granola mixture into a deep ungreased baking pan.
5. Bake 1 hour or until dry. Stir occasionally to keep granola from burning.
6. Makes an excellent cold cereal or fruit topping. Serve with cold Pear Milk (see page 49).

Crepes

½	cup	rolled oats
½	cup	whole wheat flour
1	cup	milk (soy, millet, tofu or nut)
½	ring	dried pineapple (optional)
½	cup	milk (soy, millet, tofu or nut)
1	tsp	salt
¼	tsp	vanilla to taste
¼	tsp	maple flavoring to taste

Makes 9 medium crepes

Step 3

1. Place oats, flour, pineapple and 1 cup of milk in blender jar and soak over night.
2. Next morning, add salt, vanilla, maple flavor and ½ cup of milk to soaked blender mixture. Blend all ingredients until a smooth batter forms.
3. Preheat a non-stick griddle or skillet to medium heat. Drop ⅓ cup of crepe batter onto skillet surface and immediately roll pan to spread batter evenly.
4. Cook crepe until edges begin to brown. The top must be dry before turning to brown the other side.
5. When cooked, quickly tip and slide crepe from pan onto a flat plate. Repeat this process until the batter is gone. Stack crepes on top of each other.
6. Fill the center of each crepe with fresh fruit or canned fruit. Roll up and sprinkle with chopped walnuts.

French Toast — Version #1

½ lb   medium tofu, rinsed and drained

½ cups   water

1 tbsp   honey

1 tsp   vanilla or maple flavoring

¼ tsp   salt

8 slices whole wheat bread

Serves 4 to 6

Step 3

1. Preheat a non-stick griddle or fry pan to a medium heat.
2. Place all ingredients **except bread** in blender and blend together until very smooth. Pour mixture into a bowl large enough to dip bread slices.
3. Dip into the batter as many slices of bread as your griddle surface will hold at one time. Make sure bread slices are evenly coated on both sides.
4. Place slices on oiled griddle or fry pan and brown on both sides. Repeat dipping and cooking until all slices are used.
5. Serve immediately with Corn Butter (see page 109)and your favorite jams, syrups or Thickened Fruit (see page 39).

Step 4

French Toast — Version #2

1	cup	soaked and drained garbanzo beans
⅔	cup	water
1	cup	soy or nut milk
½	tsp	salt
2	tbsp	brown sugar (optional)
1	tsp	vanilla or maple flavoring to taste
8		slices whole wheat bread

1. Preheat a non-stick griddle or fry pan to a medium heat.
2. Place all ingredients except bread in blender and blend together until very smooth. Pour mixture into a bowl large enough to dip bread slices.
3. Dip into batter as many slices of bread as your griddle surface will hold at one time. Make sure bread slices are evenly coated on both sides.
4. Place slices on griddle or fry pan and brown on both sides. Repeat dipping and cooking until all slices are used.
5. Serve immediately with Corn Butter (see page 109) and your favorite jams, syrups or Thickened Fruit (see page 39).

Serves 4 to 6

To prepare garbanzos, soak ½ cup garbanzos in 1 cup water overnight and drain.

Scrambled Tofu

1	lb	medium tofu
2	tbsp	chicken-style seasoning
¼	tsp	turmeric (optional)
¼	tsp	onion powder
salt to taste		

1. Crumble tofu into a non-stick skillet.
2. Add seasonings. Some brands of chicken-style seasoning are stronger than others. Do a taste test before you add the second tablespoon. Cook on a medium heat for 15 minutes or until crispy brown. Stir occasionally while cooking.
3. Serve on toast with *Baco Bits* and green onion.

Serves 4

To avoid "sloppy" scrambled tofu, rinse tofu, place in a colander and drain overnight in the fridge.

Rice or Millet Breakfast Pudding

2	cups	cooked rice or millet
¼	cup	dates or raisins
¼	tsp	cinnamon
¼	cup	dried or fresh chopped pineapple (optional)
½	cup	raw cashews
⅔	cup	or enough water to blend
1	tbsp	honey or maple syrup

1. Preheat oven to 350°.
2. Mix rice or millet, dates or raisins, cinnamon and pineapple in a large bowl.
3. Blend cashews, water and honey until creamy.
4. Add blended ingredients to rice mixture and combine well.
5. Place in a well-oiled casserole dish and bake for 30 minutes.
6. Serve warm with Pear Milk (see page 49) and granola.

Makes 6 half cup servings

To save time in the morning, make pudding the night before and store in the refrigerater.

Thickened Fruit

1. Thaw frozen fruit. Save the juice.
2. Drain the juice (from either canned or frozen fruit) into a small saucepan. Place saved fruit in a bowl.
3. To sweeten fruit juice, add about ⅓ cup honey for every 4 cups of fruit. (You can use concentrated grape or apple juice instead of honey. Add 1 cup of concentrate for every 4 cups of fruit.)
4. In a cup or bowl, measure out ½ cup water. Add to water 1 tbsp of cornstarch for every 1 cup of saved fruit. Stir until dissolved.
5. Bring the sweetened fruit juice to a slow boil. Add cornstarch mixture and stir constantly until liquid turns clear.
6. Remove from heat and pour over the saved fruit
7. Use as a base for fruit crisp desserts. Serve hot or cold over waffles, Crepes (see page 36) or French Toast (see page 37 or 38).

Can be made from any unsweetened, frozen or canned fruit. If you prefer the presweetened fruit, do not add extra sweetener.

Baked Apples

4 to 6	small cooking apples (any variety)
1 cup	pitted dates, cooked in a little water until soft
1 recipe	Grandma Smith's Pastry (see page 142)

Serves 4 to 6

Step 2

1. Preheat oven to 350°.
2. Wash and peel apples. Use an apple corer or knife to core out the apples.
3. Loosely fill apple centers with date filling.
4. Roll pastry dough out until thin. Cut dough into circles large enough to fit completely around and cover filled apples.
5. Place pastry-covered apples in a shallow baking dish and bake for 45 minutes or until pastry is golden brown.
6. Serve hot.

Crisp Topping

1	cup	rolled oats
½	cup	unbleached white flour
⅛	tsp	salt
½	cup	maple syrup

Serves 6

1. In a small bowl, mix above ingredients together until crumbly.
2. Pour prepared Thickened Fruit (see page 39) into an 8" x 8" cake pan.
3. Sprinkle crumbled mixture evenly over Thickened Fruit and bake at 350° for 30 minutes.

Fruit Cobbler

2	cups	unbleached white flour
¼	cup	whole wheat flour
3	tsp	baking powder
½	tsp	salt
¼	cup	brown sugar or cane sugar substitute
3	tbsp	commercial cashew butter
1¼	cups	cold tofu milk
½	tsp	vanilla

Serves 6

Step 3

1. Preheat oven to 350°.
2. Mix dry ingredients together in small bowl.
3. Cut nut butter into dry ingredients until crumbly.
4. Add milk and vanilla and combine well.
5. Pour prepared Thickened Fruit (see page 39) into an 8" x 8" cake pan.
6. Spoon cobbler mixture on top of thickened fruit and bake for 1 hour.
7. Serve hot or cold.

Opposite Page

Following Page

Milks & Jams

The Calcium Myth

by Phil Brewer

Drinking milk every day is considered a North American necessity. In order to satisfy the perceived need for calcium, most people faithfully consume dairy products even though they may not care for them. Some of the women who come to our Guest House are consuming up to 1,400 milligrams of calcium a day in an effort to ensure that their bones will remain strong throughout their retirement years.

What's behind our fixation on drinking milk for calcium? Why do North Americans think they need twice as much calcium as people in other countries? The Chinese, for instance, have virtually no dairy industry, yet they have very few cases of osteoporosis and rely mainly on plant foods as their major source of calcium.

There is a direct relationship between the amount of protein (especially animal proteins) we consume and the amount of calcium the body needs to excrete the excess acid produced from the protein break down. The North American meat-eating population typically exceeds, by two to three times, the recommended daily allowance for protein. This over-consumption of protein makes calcium supplementing a necessity. Shifting to a vegetarian diet reduces protein intake and correspondingly decreases the need for high amounts of calcium.

After eliminating the need for milk, you may find that you still want and enjoy a little milk on your favorite granola or cereal. Pear Milk (see page 49) is a great milk substitute and a Guest House favorite. Each year we preserve about 1,500 pounds of pears to make our pear milk and pear ice creams. You may also want to try experimenting with a few of the many varieties of soy milks or tofu milk products now available.

Raspberry Jam—No Sugar

1   cup   fresh or frozen unsweetened
           raspberries
2   rings dried pineapple

Yields about 2 cups

1. Wash fresh raspberries or thaw frozen raspberries.
2. Cut pineapple rings into small pieces.
3. Combine raspberries with pineapple pieces and let sit until pineapple is quite soft. If you are using frozen berries, you may have to let the fruit sit for about 8 hours to soften the pineapple.
4. Scoop fruit into blender and blend until smooth. Place jam into serving containers.

Grandma's Old-fashioned Raspberry Jam

6   cups fresh or frozen, unsweetened
            raspberries
1   tbsp lemon juice
3   cups granulated white sugar

Yields about 4 cups

P

This jam has a long shelf life.

1. Wash fresh raspberries or thaw frozen raspberries.
2. Put raspberries and lemon juice into a large sauce pan and bring to a rolling boil. Boil mixture for 2 minutes.
3. Add sugar and bring to a second rolling boil. Boil 3 minutes.
4. Remove from heat and whip jam with wire whisk or electric mixer for 5 minutes. Pour jam into serving containers.
5. If canning, put jam into jars and seal using the open kettle method. Keeps for 2 to 3 months.

Strawberry Jam

| 1 | cup | fresh or frozen, unsweetened strawberries |
| 1 | ring | dried pineapple |

Yields 2 cups.
Keeps about 1
week in the fridge

1. Wash fresh strawberries or thaw and drain frozen strawberries.
2. Cut pineapple rings into small pieces.
3. Combine strawberries with pineapple pieces and let sit overnight or until pineapple is quite soft. If you are using frozen berries, you may have to let the fruit sit for about 8 hours to soften the pineapple.
4. Scoop fruit into blender and blend until smooth. Place jam into serving containers.
5. Chill and serve with your favorite breads.

Tropical Jam

1	cup	dried pineapple pieces
½	cup	dried papaya pieces
⅔	cup	pineapple juice or orange juice

Yields 2 cups

1. Combine dried fruit pieces in a bowl. Pour enough juice to cover fruit and let stand overnight or about 8 hours.
2. Drain fruit, reserving juice. Scoop fruit into blender and blend until smooth. Add reserved fruit juice to blender and continue blending until jam is smooth.
3. Place jam into serving containers.
4. Chill and serve.
5. For variation combine dried apricots with the dried pineapple pieces. Keeps about one week in the fridge.

Marmalade

½ cup grated fresh orange peel
1 cup orange pulp
½ fresh lemon, thinly sliced with peel
1½ cups water
3 cups dried pineapple pieces
⅓ cup water

Yields 4 cups

1. Place orange peel, orange pulp and lemon slices in a large pot. Add 1½ cups water and simmer for 5 minutes.
2. Cover pot and let mixture stand in a cool place for 12 hours.
3. Return to heat and cook rapidly for about 30 minutes or until peel is tender.
4. Put dried pineapple and ⅓ cup of water in a small bowl. Cook in microwave for 2 minutes at a time until fruit is soft enough to blend. Pour pineapple into blender and blend until smooth.
5. Add blended pineapple to orange and lemon in saucepan, bring to a boil and simmer for 15 minutes.
6. Spoon into containers, chill and serve with your favorite breads.

Pear Milk

½ cup raw cashews or blanched almonds
¼ tsp salt
1 tsp vanilla
1 tsp honey (optional)
1 quart canned pears
1 cup water or pear juice

Makes 4 cups

1. Place nuts in blender. Add water or pear juice and blend until very smooth. Do not underblend.
2. Add remaining ingredients to blender and continue blending until you have a thick, smooth consistency. Add more water or pear juice if necessary.
3. Chill well. Serve with hot cereals and granola or pour over Thickened Fruit (see page 39).

Millet Milk

⅔   cup   hot cooked millet
⅓   cup   raw cashews
1   tsp   vanilla
1   tsp   salt
1   tbsp honey
3   cups water

1. Place cashews in blender. Add 1 of the 3 cups of water and blend until very smooth. Do not underblend.
2. Add remaining ingredients to blender and continue blending until you have a smooth pouring consistency. Add more water if necessary.
3. Chill well and serve in place of regular milk.

Makes 4 cups

TP

Use white vanilla in all your milks, ice creams and cream sauces. It will help keep them white.

Entrées

Protein

by Phil Brewer

During the past two years, the North American Food Guides have been largely rewritten with grains replacing meats and dairy products as the number one food group. However, the old ideas with respect to protein are much harder to debunk. Concepts such as complete proteins, the necessity of animal proteins, and the need for food combining to include all of the essential amino acids are still sacred cows. It is going to take a considerable amount of re-education to convince several generations of meat-eaters to develop new dietary habits.

Our bodies do need protein. It is an essential ingredient to good physical health. However, the question of how much protein we need varies. Studies indicate that the average, non-vegetarian North American consumes over 100 grams of protein a day, much of it in the form of animal protein. In order to breakdown these high quantities of protein, the liver and kidneys are forced to work harder. As your protein intake rises, so does the amount of calcium excreted in the urine. If you eat the typical high protein diet, this calcium loss may affect the density of your bones and lead to osteoporosis. The result, people who consume meat, eggs and milk every day are much more susceptible to a variety of diseases including liver and kidney disease, cancer, arthritis and osteoporosis.

Our recommended daily allowance has provided us with some guidelines on daily protein requirements. It recommends 46 grams a day for the average woman and 56 grams (or 2 ounces) a day for the average man. A vegetarian diet will provide you with a more than adequate intake of protein, without the unwanted fat or cholesterol contained in meat and dairy products. Here is a sample of the protein contained in the following foods:

1 cup of pinto beans	15	grams
1 baked potato	5	grams
1 cup of asparagus	5	grams
2 slices whole wheat bread	6	grams
1 cup of broccoli	6	grams
1 cup of green peas	8	grams

Moving to a diet based on vegetable rather than animal protein requires more than eliminating meat from the menu. Learning to develop a balanced menu based soley on grains, vegetables and fruits often takes time and practice. Most North American cooks plan their meals around an entree dish that traditionally involves a selection from the animal kingdom. However, these meat, chicken or fish entrees are loaded not only with excessive amounts of animal protein but also with 30% to 70% fat and extremely high levels of cholesterol. On the other hand, grain-based entrees will provide you with complex carbohydrates, dietary fiber and important vitamins and minerals without saturating your system with fat and cholesterol.

The recipes in this section contain a variety of tasty wheat, oat, rice, barley and millet dishes that can easily serve as the centerpiece of your meals. Try a few. Our non-vegetarian health guests are often amazed that meals without a meat, chicken or fish main course can be so delicious and satisfying. You may be too.

Walnut Rice Loaf

2	cups	whole wheat bread crumbs
2	cups	cooked brown rice
1	cup	chopped walnuts
1	med.	onion chopped fine
2	stalks	celery, chopped fine
1	tbsp	chopped parsley (fresh or dried)
½	tsp	salt
1	cup	raw cashews
¼	cup	soy sauce
¾	cup	water

Serves 4 to 6

TP

If your loaf mixture seems too sloppy, add a little more rice or bread crumbs; if it's too dry, add a little more water.

1. Combine bread crumbs, rice, walnuts, onion, celery, parsley and salt in a large bowl and mix well.
2. Place cashews, soy sauce and water into a blender and blend until smooth.
3. Pour blended mixture over loaf mixture and mix thoroughly.
4. Preheat oven to 350°.
5. Press mixture into an 8" x 8" lightly oiled baking pan. Bake for 30 minutes or until top turns to a golden crust.

Angela's Unsausage

1	cup	water
2	tbsp	soy sauce
1	cup	quick oats
1	tbsp	oil
1	tsp	honey
1	tsp	onion powder
½	tsp	sage
1	tbsp	yeast flakes
¼	tsp	garlic powder
⅛	tsp	Italian seasoning

Makes 10 sausages

1. Combine water and seasoning in a two quart saucepan and bring to boil. Add oats and cook for 5-10 minutes.
2. Cool slightly and form into sausages. Bake at 350° for 15 minutes on each side on an oiled cookie sheet.

Cashew Rice Loaf

1	cup	finely ground raw cashews	Serves 4 to 6
1	med.	cooking onion finely diced	
1	cup	soft whole wheat bread crumbs	
¾	cup	tofu or nut milk	
1	cup	cooked brown rice	
2	tbsp	soy sauce	
½	tsp	salt or to taste	
1	tbsp	dried or fresh parsley	
¼	tsp	celery salt	

1. Thoroughly mix all ingredients together in a large bowl.
2. Lightly pack mixture in an oiled small loaf pan and bake at 350° for approximately 40 minutes or until loaf is firm.
3. Turn out of pan onto a serving dish. Garnish with cranberry sauce and fresh parsley. Serve with mashed potatoes and Chicken Gravy (see page 106).

Lentil Loaf

½	cup	ground sunflower seeds	Serves 4 to 6
1	cup	cooked brown lentils	
¼	cup	cooked brown rice	
¼	cup	whole wheat bread crumbs	
½	cup	canned tomatoes cut in pieces	
⅓	cup	finely diced raw onion	
⅓	cup	finely diced celery	
1	tsp	salt	
⅛	tsp	sage	
1	tbsp	yeast flakes	
½	tbsp	chicken style seasoning	
3	tbsp	tomato paste	

1. Thoroughly mix all ingredients together in a large bowl.
2. Lightly pack mixture into an oiled 4" x 8" loaf pan and bake at 350° for 40 minutes or until brown.
3. Turn out of pan and cut into ½" serving slices.
4. Serve with your favorite potato and vegetable.

Walnut Burgers

1	cup	whole wheat bread crumbs
1	cup	cooked brown rice
⅔	cup	ground walnuts
½	cup	diced raw onion
½	cup	finely diced celery
½	cup	quick oats (uncooked)
1	tsp	dried parsley flakes
¼	cup	raw cashew pieces
¼	cup	soy sauce
½	cup	medium tofu
1	tbsp	gluten flour or garbanzo flour
½	tsp	salt
¼	cup	water as needed

Makes 10 large burgers

To freeze, partially fry burgers on both sides, cool and then freeze. To cook, thaw in microwave and finish frying until brown.

1. Sauté onions in a non-stick or lightly oiled pan.
2. In a large bowl, combine bread crumbs, rice, walnuts, onions, celery, oats and parsley and mix well. Set aside.
3. Pour cashews, soy sauce and tofu into a blender along with enough water to keep blending until extremely smooth.
4. Add gluten flour to blender and pulse the blender for several seconds.
5. Add sautéed onions, salt and blended liquid to bread crumb mixture and mix well.
6. Using a ¼ cup scoop, wax paper and a large jar ring, form into patties about ½" thick. Place in a lightly oiled or non-stick fry pan and cook both sides until brown.
7. Serve with burger buns and garnishes.

Millet Patties

¾	cup	cooked millet
½	cup	mashed potatoes
¼	cup	quick rolled oats (uncooked)
½	cup	ground nuts (walnuts, cashews or almonds)
½	cup	diced raw onion
¼	cup	water
½	tsp	salt
1	tbsp	chicken style seasoning
1 ½	tbsp	nutritional yeast

Makes 8 medium patties

1. Mix all ingredients together in a large bowl.
2. Using a ¼ cup scoop, form into patties about ½" thick. Place in a lightly oiled or non-stick fry pan and cook both sides until brown.
3. Place patties in a lightly oiled shallow baking dish and cover with your favorite gravy or tomato sauce. Bake at 350° for 30 minutes.
4. Can also be served plain with burger buns and burger garnishes.

Cabbage Rolls

1   large loose cabbage
6   cups water
1   tsp salt
1   Cabbage Roll Filling recipe
    (see page 59)
2   cups tomato sauce or tomato soup

Makes 18 large
cabbage rolls

Step 2

Step 2

Prepare cabbage on stovetop:
1. In a large pot, add salt and water and
   bring to a boil.
2. Place large cabbage leaves in boiling water
   for about 1 minute to make them tender.
   Remove from water. Shave away part of
   each leaf's thick central rib so it will roll
   easily.

Or, prepare cabbage in microwave:
1. Core and wash cabbage and place it in a
   plastic bag.
2. Microwave on high, in 2 to 3 minute
   bursts, or until the leaves are tender. Remove leaves as they soften.

Stuff and wrap cabbage leaves:
1. Preheat oven to 350°.
2. Put a good spoonful of prepared Cabbage
   Roll Filling on the stem end of each leaf.
   Fold the leaf end and sides over the stuffing. Roll up the leaf from the stem end to
   make a neat parcel.
3. Carefully place the rolls in a large, lightly
   oiled casserole dish with the free ends of
   the leaves on the bottom. Pack them
   snugly together so that they cannot un-
   roll.
4. Cover the rolls with your favorite tomato
   sauce or tomato soup.
5. Cover the casserole dish and bake for
   about 90 minutes at 325°.
6. Serve hot with Four Bean Salad (see page
   92) and sauerkraut.

Cabbage Roll Filling

1	large	cooking onion finely diced
1	cup	finely diced celery
1	cup	raw cashews
1⅔	cups	water
2	tbsp	chicken style seasoning
1	tsp	salt
4	cups	cooked rice
½	cup	uncooked cornmeal (optional)
1	cup	ground gluten (optional)

Stuffs about 18 large cabbage rolls

1. Sauté onion and celery in a lightly oiled skillet until tender.
2. Pour cashews in a blender, add 1 cup of water and blend until smooth. Add remaining water, seasoning and salt to blender and blend for another minute.
3. Add blended mixture to sautéed onions and celery, heat and stir until bubbling.
4. In a large bowl, combine rice, cornmeal and gluten. Pour cooked sauce over dry ingredients and mix well.
5. Spoon filling onto prepared cabbage leaves, roll up and bake as directed in Cabbage Roll recipe (see page 58).

Bread Dressing

3	cups	cubed whole wheat bread, slightly toasted
1½	tsp	sage
1	tbsp	chicken style seasoning
1	tbsp	nutritional yeast
⅔	cup	raw cashews
⅔	cup	water
½	tsp	salt
1	tbsp	chicken style seasoning
½	cup	diced celery
½	cup	diced raw onion
1	tsp	olive oil

Great addition to a Thanksgiving or Christmas dinner. Serves 4 to 6

1. Mix bread cubes, sage, chicken seasoning and yeast together in a large bowl. Set aside.
2. Pour cashews and remaining seasonings into blender. Add water and blend until very smooth.
3. Add olive oil to fry pan and sauté celery and onion pieces until soft.
4. Add blended mixture to pan with sautéed celery and onions and bring liquid to a boil.
5. Pour liquid over bread cubes. Mix thoroughly.
6. Preheat oven to 350°.
7. Place bread cubes in an oiled 8" x 8" casserole dish and bake for 30 to 40 minutes.
8. Serve with cranberries and gravy.

Opposite Page

Tillie's Potatoes—page 85
Irish Stew—page 68 & Rye Bread—page 29
Cashew Rice Loaf—page 55
Chicken Gravy—page 106

Tofu Croquettes

⅓	cup	minced onion
1	tbsp	olive oil
½	lb	medium tofu drained, rinsed and blended smooth
1½	cups	soft whole wheat bread crumbs
½	cup	ground walnuts
1	tbsp	chicken style seasoning
1	tbsp	yeast flakes
½	tsp	sage
½	tsp	salt

1. Sauté onion in olive oil until soft. Place in a medium bowl.
2. Add all remaining ingredients to sautéed onion and combine well.
3. Place mixture in refrigerator and allow to chill for 1 hour.
4. Use a ¼ cup ice cream scoop to form batter into croquette balls.
5. Place croquettes on an oiled baking dish. Bake at 350° for 20 to 30 minutes or until brown.
6. Before serving, cover the baked croquettes with your favorite gravy and bake at 350° for another 20 or 30 minutes.

Makes 8 to 10 medium-sized croquettes

TP

Tofu croquettes freeze well. Prepare ahead and then thaw only the amount you need for your meal.

Opposite Page

Pinapple Cheesecake—page 139
Betty's Gluten Burger and Broth—page 69

Fish Sticks

2	cups	water
1	cup	quick oats
3	cups	Cottage Cheese (see page 94)
¾	cup	Flaxseed Gel (see page 111)
1	tsp	salt
1	cup	cracker crumbs
1	cup	diced onions
2	tbsp	chicken style seasoning

1. Cook oats in water for 5 minutes.
2. In a large bowl, mix tofu, Flaxseed Gel, cracker crumbs, onions and seasoning. Add oatmeal and combine well.
3. Spread mixture evenly on a well oiled cookie sheet. Bake at 275° for 45 minutes.
4. Let baked mixture sit in the fridge over night to thicken.
5. Slice mixture into 2" x 4" strips. (Freeze at this point if you wish).
6. Dip thawed sticks in Cornflake Breading Mix (see page 64) taking care to coat all sides thoroughly and evenly.
7. In a non-stick or lightly oiled fry pan, cook fish sticks slowly, over medium heat, until golden brown on both sides.
8. Serve hot with lemon wedges, Tartar Sauce (see page 108), potato wedges or french fries.

Makes 20 sticks

TP

If cornflake crumbs refuse to adhere, first dip quickly in soy milk and then in crumb mixture.

Cornflake Breading

2	cups	finely crushed cornflakes
1	tsp	onion powder

salt to taste

1. Mix ingredients in a shallow bowl.
2. Use as a breading for any recipes that require a breading mix such as Fish Sticks (see page 64).

Ingrid's Walnut Balls

1   cup   dry whole wheat bread crumbs
½   cup   Cottage Cheese (see page 94)
1   med. onion diced fine
½   tsp   sage
½   cup   ground walnuts
⅔   cup   Flaxseed Gel (see page 111)
salt to taste

1. Mix all ingredients together in a large bowl and combine well.
2. Form mixture into small balls, approximately 1" diameter.
3. Over medium heat sauté balls until evenly brown all around.

Makes 24 small balls

Do not put balls into a spaghetti sauce as they will crumble. Best served as a side dish to spaghetti pasta.

Stroganoff

1   cup   diced onion
1   cup   diced celery
1   cup   diced green or red pepper (optional)
1½ cup   raw cashews
3   cups water
½   tsp   garlic powder
1   tsp   celery salt
2   tbsp beef or chicken style seasoning
1   tsp   soy sauce
salt to taste
2   cups prepared Marinated Gluten Strips ground (see page 66)

1. Sauté onions, celery and peppers.
2. Blend cashews in 1 cup of water until creamy and smooth. Add remaining water and seasonings to blender.
3. Pour into sautéed vegetables and bring to a boil, stirring constantly.
4. Add prepared ground gluten and cook until hot.
5. Serve over brown rice or pasta noodles.

Marinated Gluten Strips

⅔	cup	soy beans
⅔	cup	walnuts
1	tbsp	garlic powder or 3 crushed garlic cloves
1	large	onion, chopped
2	cups	water
3	cups	gluten flour
¾	cup	unbleached white flour
1	tsp	olive oil

1. Place soy beans in enough water to cover and let soak overnight.
2. Drain, add fresh water and boil in a small pot for 15 minutes. Drain and cool.
3. Place cooked soy beans, walnuts, garlic and onion in a blender. Add 2 cups water and blend until smooth.
4. In a large bowl, combine gluten flour and unbleached flour. Pour in blended liquid and mix quickly to make a dough.
5. Form dough into 8 large patties about ¾" thick.
6. Add olive oil to fry pan and brown patties on both sides. Freeze the patties.
7. Thaw, slice, cook and marinate (see Gluten Marinade on page 67) only the number of patties you will need for your meal or recipe. When sliced, the 8 frozen patties should yield about 10 cups of thin gluten strips or about 1¼ cup gluten slices per pattie.

Can be used in place of beef in recipes that call for chipped beef or beef strips. Makes 8 large patties or about 25 servings.

To save time, double the amount of soy beans you cook for this recipe. Freeze the excess beans and use them in your next recipe.

For quicker accessibility, slice all 8 frozen patties into thin strips. Fry up gluten strips (on both sides) and refreeze them. Then thaw and marinate only the amount of strips you will need for your meal or recipe.

Gluten Marinade

2 frozen patties or 2 cups gluten strips
1 clove crushed garlic
⅓ cup soy sauce
⅓ cup water
¼ cup chopped onion and/or green pepper

Makes enough to marinate cooked strips from 2 frozen patties or 2 cups thawed gluten strips.

1. While still slightly frozen, cut the patties into very thin strips and fry again on both sides in a non-stick or oil-sprayed pan. Or thaw 5 cups pre-fried gluten strips. Place in a large bowl.
2. Combine garlic, soy sauce, water and onion/green pepper in a small bowl. Pour over gluten strips and let stand for an hour. If you prefer a stronger flavor, allow gluten to marinate longer.
3. Place strips and sauce into a fry pan and simmer until warm and liquid is absorbed.
4. Once gluten strips have been fried twice and marinated, they are ready to be used in your recipes or as a side dish. Marinated gluten strips can also be ground up and used in place of hamburger in your favorite stroganoff, chili, cabbage roll or lasagna recipes.

Irish Stew

6 small potatoes
1 small turnip (optional)
2 med. carrots
2 stalks celery
1 med. onion, coarsely chopped
1 cup frozen or fresh peas
1 cup prepared Marinated Gluten
     Strips (see page 66)
1 recipe Mary's Brown Gravy
     (see page 106)

Serves 4

1. Peel potatoes, turnips and carrots. Cut all vegetables into fairly large pieces.
2. Parboil potato and turnip pieces together in one pot. Parboil carrot and celery pieces together in another. Do not cook these two groups in the same pot. Drain and set aside.
3. Sauté onion in a lightly oiled pan until tender.
4. Arrange prepared gluten, parboiled vegetables, onions and peas in the bottom of a deep, oiled roasting pan.
5. Pour prepared gravy over top, cover and bake at 350° for 40 minutes.
6. Serve with hot crusty rolls or rye bread. You can also use this recipe as a pot pie filler.

Betty's Gluten Burgers

1	cup	gluten flour
1	cup	quick oats
¼	cup	yeast flakes
¼	cup	soy flour
¼	cup	wheat germ
1	tbsp	chicken or beef style seasoning
1	tsp	thyme
1	tsp	sage
1	med.	onion diced fine
2	cloves	garlic diced fine
1½	cups	hot water
3	tbsp	olive oil
¼	cup	soy sauce

Makes 12 medium burgers

1. Combine dry ingredients and thoroughly mix.
2. In a large bowl, mix onion, garlic, hot water, olive oil and soy sauce.
3. Add dry ingredients to liquid. Mix well and let stand 3 to 5 minutes.
4. Form into burger-sized patties. Place in a lightly oiled or non-stick pan and fry both sides until brown. Place burgers in a shallow casserole or baking pan. Set aside and prepare the following broth recipe.

Broth for Betty's Gluten Burgers

2½	cups	water
½	cup	soy sauce
1	tbsp	yeast flakes
1	tbsp	chicken style seasoning
¼	cup	chopped onion
garlic to taste		

Makes enough broth to cover one recipe of Betty's Gluten Burgers

1. Combine all ingredients in a small bowl. Pour over gluten burger patties.
2. Cover pan with lid or tin foil and bake at 350° for 1 hour.
3. Serve hot with potatoes and your favorite vegetables.

Stir Fry Vegetables

1	lb	medium tofu, drained and rinsed
2	tbsp	chicken style seasoning
⅔	cup	carrots
1	cup	cauliflower
⅔	cup	celery
1	cup	broccoli
¼	cup	bean sprouts
⅔	cup	edible pod peas
1 10 oz		can water chestnuts (optional)
1 10 oz		can baby corn cobs (optional)
⅔	cup	bok choy
1	tbsp	olive oil
¼	cup	water

Serves 4 to 6

For a different flavor, use 1 tbsp sesame oil instead of olive oil for stir fry vegetables.

1. Cut tofu into bite-size cubes. Place in non-stick or oiled frying pan and sprinkle with chicken seasoning. Brown evenly and set aside.
2. Cut carrots, cauliflower, celery and broccoli into medium, bite-sized pieces.
3. Put olive oil in the bottom of a wok or similar thick bottomed pot.
4. Turn on high and let oil heat up. Add vegetables in the order listed. Allow each one to partially cook before adding the next. Stir several times after each addition.
5. If the vegetables begin to brown instead of steam, add water, 1 tablespoon at a time. Add browned tofu cubes and stir quickly to reheat tofu.
6. Serve immediately. Goes great with other Oriental style foods.

Fried Rice

⅓ cup   finely diced raw onion   Serves 4
¼ cup   finely diced carrot
¼ cup   finely diced celery
4 cups cooked brown rice
⅓ cup   peas (fresh or thawed)
1 tbsp soy sauce
2 tbsp chicken style seasoning

1. Sauté onion, carrot and celery with a little olive oil in the bottom of a wok or similar thick bottomed pan.
2. Add rice, peas, soy sauce and seasoning. Mix and thoroughly heat all ingredients in pan.
3. Serve with Stir Fried Vegetables (see page 70) and Egg Rolls (see page 72).

Sweet & Sour Tofu

1 lb   medium tofu   Serves 6
¼ cup   soy sauce
¼ cup   water
¼ cup   cornstarch
1 recipe Sweet & Sour Sauce
         (see page 107)

1. Rinse and drain tofu. Cut tofu into ½" cubes.
2. In a small bowl, mix soy sauce, water and cornstarch.
3. Dip tofu cubes into soy sauce mixture making sure all sides are evenly coated.
4. Place cubes in a non-stick or oiled fry pan over medium heat. Cook until brown on all sides.
5. Put cubes in an oiled 8" x 8" casserole pan and pour Sweet and Sour Sauce mixture over top.
6. Serve with Stir Fried Vegetables (see page 70) and rice.

Egg Rolls

1	lb	medium tofu, drained and rinsed
¼	cup	chicken style seasoning
½	cup	finely diced onion
1	cup	shredded cabbage
⅓	cup	finely diced carrot
½	cup	finely diced celery
8	sheets	thawed filo/strudel pastry leaves

1. In a large bowl, crumble tofu together with chicken seasoning. Then sauté in a non-stick or lightly oiled frying pan until golden brown. Remove from pan and return to bowl.
2. Sauté each of the vegetables separately in a lightly oiled fry pan.
3. Add sautéed vegetables to tofu mixture and combine well.
4. Preheat oven to 375°.
5. Place two sheets of filo/strudel pastry on counter top.
6. Put 1 cup of egg roll mixture along one edge of the pastry sheets and roll up. Then cut roll into 2" pieces to yield approximately 5 egg rolls per roll.
7. Place egg rolls on a non-stick cookie sheet. Brush lightly with olive oil and bake for 20 minutes or until golden brown.
8. Serve hot with Fried Rice (see page 71) and Stir Fry Vegetables (see page 70).

Yields 24 medium egg rolls

T🔻P

Keep filo pastry covered with plastic wrap as much as possible as it tends to dry very quickly.

Baked Brown Beans

2	cups	dry navy beans
1	large	cooking onion sliced
½	tsp	garlic powder or 1 clove fresh garlic diced
4	cups	tomato juice or blended canned tomatoes
½	cup	unbleached white flour
3	tbsp	maple syrup or honey
3	tbsp	molasses
1½	tsp	salt
½	cup	tomato paste
1	tbsp	lemon juice
½	tsp	celery salt

Serves 8

P

For variety, try adding 2 tablespoons hot mustard or 1 cup sliced veggie wieners to beans before baking.

1. Soak dry beans over night in 6 cups of water. Drain and rinse with cold water.
2. Place beans in a large saucepan. Add 6 cups water, cover and cook 2 ½ to 3 hours or until beans are soft. Drain and set aside.
3. Sauté onion and garlic with a little olive oil in the bottom of a 2-quart saucepan.
4. Add 3 cups of the tomato juice and bring to a boil.
5. Pour remaining 1 cup tomato juice and flour into blender and blend until smooth. Add blended juice to saucepan.
6. Reduce heat to low and add all remaining ingredients. Simmer for 10 minutes.
7. Place drained, cooked beans in a large lightly oiled casserole dish. Pour tomato sauce over beans, stir and cover. Bake slowly at 350° for 1½ to 2 hours.
8. Serve with Rye Bread (see page 29) and tossed green salad.

Pinto Beans

1	cup	dry pinto beans
2 ½	cups	water (add more as needed)
1	med.	cooking onion sliced fine
2	cloves	garlic minced
3	tbsp	beef style seasoning
½	tsp	cummin
½	tsp	paprika
1	small	jalapeno pepper cut fine (optional)

salt to taste

1. Soak dry beans in 3 cups of hot water for at least 6 hours.
2. Drain and rinse with cold water.
3. Place beans in a large saucepan. Add 2 ½ cups water, cover and cook about 2 hours or until beans are soft.
4. Sauté onion slices in a little olive oil. Add to cooked beans.
5. Add garlic, jalapeno, seasonings and salt. Simmer slowly for 30 minutes.
6. Serve with corn chips and vegetables. Mash leftover beans and serve as refried beans.

Great as is or re-heat and serve as refried beans.
Serves 6

To have a refried bean style dish, mash half of your pinto beans after they have sim-mered for 30 min-utes and place them in a baking dish. Bake for 30 minutes.

Taco Salads or "Haystacks"

4	cups	of your favorite corn chips
4	cups	warm refried beans
2	cups	shredded lettuce
2		tomatoes diced
½		long English cucumber diced
1	10 oz	can sliced black olives
½	cup	Tofu Mayonnaise (see page 96)
½	cup	shredded soy cheese
½	cup	your favorite salsa
½	cup	Guacamole (see page 110)

Serves 4

1. Begin forming your haystack by placing 1 cup of corn chips on each plate. Place 1 cup of refried beans on top of the corn chips.
2. Add a layer of each of the remaining ingre-dients until you have made a neat stack.
3. Serve immediately.

Spicy Chili

1	cup	chopped onion
1	clove	garlic, chopped
1	small	jalapeno pepper, diced fine
1	tbsp	olive oil
1	cup	chopped celery
1	cup	chopped green pepper
2	cups	tomato juice
2	cups	canned tomatoes
1	tsp	salt
1	tsp	cumin
⅛	tsp	cayenne
1	5½oz	can tomato paste
1	19oz	can cooked kidney beans
1½	cups	Marinated Gluten Strips (see page 66) ground up

Serves 8

1. Put olive oil into a large saucepan and sauté onion, jalapeno and garlic until glassy.
2. Add celery and peppers and stir for 1 minute. Pour in tomato juice and canned tomatoes and slowly bring to a boil.
3. Add remaining ingredients and simmer slowly for 1 hour.
4. Serve with corn chips and Baked Enchiladas (see page 76).

Spanish Rice

4	cups	cooked brown rice
3	tbsp	salsa (commercially prepared or fresh)
½	tsp	paprika
½	tsp	salt
¼	tsp	celery salt
2	stalks	celery, chopped fine

Serves 4 to 6

1. In a large bowl, mix cooked rice with salsa, seasonings and chopped celery.
2. Add a little olive oil to a deep-sided frying pan. Add rice mixture. Brown and heat thoroughly for a few minutes.
3. Serve hot with tacos or burritos.

Baked Enchiladas

1 28 oz		can Tomatillos	Serves 8
3		Serrano chili peppers	
1	small	handful cilantro	
1	tsp	salt	
1	tsp	olive oil	
1½	cups	water	
1	cup	Soy Cream Cheese (see page 101)	
18		corn flour tortillas	
¾	cup	shredded cheddar-flavored soy cheese	
1½	cups	chopped lettuce	
¾	cup	shredded mozzarella-flavored soy cheese	
¼	cup	chopped cilantro	
¼	cup	finely chopped red pepper	
¼	cup	finely chopped green pepper	
1	med.	avocado (optional)	

1. Drain tomatillos and place tomatillos, serrano chilies, small handful of cilantro, salt, olive oil and water in blender. Blend until almost smooth.
2. Pour blended tomatillos salsa mixture into a heavy bottomed saucepan and bring to a slow boil. Remove from heat.
3. Pour ¾ cup of the cooked tomatillos salsa on the bottom of an oiled 8" x 12" casserole dish. Cover salsa with one layer of corn tortillas. Pour another ½ cup of tomatillos salsa on top of tortillas. Cover salsa with another layer of corn tortillas. Continue layering tomatillos salsa and corn tortillas until you have a 1" thick casserole ending with a layer of corn tortillas.
4. Spread Soy Cream Cheese over the final layer of tortillas. Sprinkle with chopped lettuce, shredded cheeses and chopped cilantro. Garnish with chopped red and green peppers.
5. Place casserole in a preheated 350° oven and bake about 15 to 20 minutes or until cheese melts.
6. Remove from oven and garnish with sliced avocado. Serve.

Tomato Pasta Sauce

1	small	cooking onion diced fine
3	cups	tomato juice
1	6 oz	can tomato paste
1	tbsp	honey
1	tsp	Italian seasoning
1	tsp	basil
½	tsp	celery salt
½	tsp	paprika
½	tsp	onion powder
1	tsp	salt (or to taste)
pinch		garlic powder or 1 garlic clove
pinch		cayenne
1	tbsp	unbleached white flour

1. Sauté onion with a little olive oil in the bottom of a 2-quart saucepan.
2. Add 2 cups of tomato juice, tomato paste, honey and all seasonings. Bring sauce to a boil at medium heat.
3. Pour remaining cup of juice into blender, add flour and blend together. Pour blender contents into saucepan.
4. Simmer on low heat for 30 minutes.
5. Ladle sauce over cooked pasta. Serve with bread rolls and green salad.

Makes 4 cups

TIP

Tomato sauces always taste better when allowed to sit in the refrigerator overnight.

Tofu Manicotti

1	lb	medium tofu, drained and mashed
3	tbsp	chicken style seasoning
1	cup	diced onion
1	cup	diced celery
2	cloves	garlic, minced (optional)
1	10 oz	package thawed frozen spinach (optional)
1	lb	dry manicotti shell pasta
2	cups	Tomato Pasta Sauce (see page 77)
½	cup	grated soy cheese

Serves 6

P

Use a pastry bag to stuff the manicotti shells.

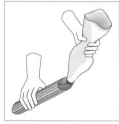

Step 6

1. In a large non-stick or oil-sprayed fry pan, sauté tofu and chicken style seasoning.
2. Add onions, celery and garlic and sauté until tender.
3. Add spinach, mix well and heat thoroughly.
4. Preheat oven to 350°.
5. Cook manicotti in the usual manner until it is partially cooked. Drain but **do not rinse pasta.**
6. Fill partially cooked shells with tofu stuffing and place in a well oiled large casserole dish.
7. Spoon tomato sauce over pasta, cover and bake for 45 minutes.
8. Uncover and sprinkle with grated cheese. Return to oven and bake until cheese melts.
9. Serve with Garlic Bread (see page 114) and Gisele's Greek Salad (see page 96).

Opposite Page

Sweet & Sour Tofu—page 71
Egg Rolls—page 72
Marinated Gluten Strips—page 66
Stir Fry Vegetables—page 70

Creamy Alfredo Sauce

½	cup	raw cashews
1¼	cups	water
1	tbsp	unbleached white flour
1	tbsp	chicken style seasoning
¼	tsp	onion powder
½	tsp	salt
1	tsp	basil
¼	cup	white soya cheese (optional)

1. Pour cashews, flour, seasoning, onion powder and salt into blender. Add water and blend until creamy.
2. Pour blended mixture into saucepan and bring to a slow boil.
3. Add basil and remove from heat.
4. Ladle over cooked fettuccine noodles and serve with steamed broccoli pieces.

Makes 3 cups

TIP

For a creamy pasta casserole pour one recipe of Creamy Alfredo Sauce over 6 cups of precooked pasta shells and bake for 30 minutes.

Gisele's Spaghetti Pizza

Serves 6

1	lb	dry spaghetti pasta
2	cups	Tomato Pasta Sauce (see page 77)
2	cups	favorite pizza toppings (sliced peppers, mushrooms, olives, onion, etc.)
1	cup	grated soy cheese

1. Cook spaghetti in usual manner until tender. Drain but do not rinse pasta.
2. Preheat oven to 425°.
3. Spread cooked pasta on a well oiled cookie sheet and bake for 15 minutes.
4. Remove from oven and cover with tomato sauce. Add your favorite pizza toppings and sprinkle evenly with grated soy cheese.
5. Reduce oven heat to 350° and bake for 30 minutes.
6. Cut into slices and serve with Garlic Bread (see page 114) and green salad.

Opposite Page

Vegetables

Why Vegetarian?

by Phil Brewer

Nutritional science is a popular and rapidly expanding field of study. Although the amount of available scientific information is staggering, one theory on food and nutrition often conflicts with another. I once asked a nutritionist who visited our Silver Hills Guest House how she was able to trust the results of nutritional studies that were funded by companies such as General Foods and other commercial food conglomerates. She agreed that there was likely to be some bias in the results of any study paid for by a vested-interest group. As well, most nutritionists now agree that performing food experiments on rats may not be the best method of learning the facts about human nutrition. If nutritional scientists are having difficulty determining the "facts" about foods, then what is the average family cook supposed to do?

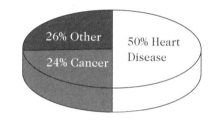

The *facts* of the matter are that, in North America, almost 50% of the annual deaths are the result of cardiovascular disease and another 24% are related to some form of cancer. Another *fact* is that the latest national food guides no longer promote the traditional "four food groups" of meat, dairy, breads and vegetables; they recommend an entirely different order of daily food servings. Grains now have first place and servings of fruits and vegetables are second. The new food guides suggest only small amounts of daily dairy servings and even smaller amounts of meats and meat substitutes. Dr. Colin Campbell, a Cornell University nutritionist and author of one of the largest studies on human nutrition, has come out in favor of a largely vegetarian diet. He cites the benefits of this type of diet in terms of higher fiber, vitamin and mineral content, lower protein and fat intake and more calories with less weight gain. Other nutritionists, as well as many medical doctors, are now beginning to recognize and endorse the healthy benefits of a vegetarian diet. Reducing the amount of dietary fat and cholesterol has been proven to reduce the risk of heart disease, cancer and many other diseases.

Converting to a vegetarian diet doesn't have to happen overnight. You can start by making one of our entree, dessert or breakfast recipes. Then add a second or third dish to your weekly menu. Buy whole grain breads instead of enriched white bread. Increase the amount of fresh fruits and vegetables you serve with your meals; reduce the number of dairy products you eat. As you use up the food items in your cupboards, replace them with ones we recommend in our Vegetarian Kitchen Starter Kit (see page 6). Remember, changing your lifestyle begins with the first successful attempt. Your family's health is worth the effort.

Tillie's Potatoes

8	cooked (but still firm) medium, whole potatoes	Serves 6
1	small onion	
⅔	cup raw cashews	
¼	tsp celery salt	
½	tsp onion powder	
¼	tsp salt	
¾	cup water	
paprika		

1. Preheat oven to 350°.
2. Grate potatoes with coarse grater and place in bowl. Grate onion with fine grater and mix together with potatoes.
3. Place cashews, celery salt and onion powder in a blender. Add water and blend until very smooth and creamy.
4. Pour blended mixture over potatoes and onions and mix together.
5. Place potatoes in an oiled 8" x 12" casserole dish. Sprinkle with paprika. Cover and bake for 45 minutes.
6. Serve with a Cashew Rice Loaf (see page 55) or other loaf.

Potato Wedges or French Fries

6	med. baking potatoes	Makes 4 servings
1	tbsp olive oil	
1	tsp salt, *Herbamare* or other herb salt	

1. Preheat oven to 450°.
2. Peel and cut potatoes into either french fry or wedge shape.
3. Place potatoes in large bowl. Toss with olive oil and salt/seasoning until potatoes are evenly coated.
4. Place on oiled cookie sheet and bake 45 minutes or until golden brown.
5. Serve hot with burgers or sandwiches and green salad. Garnish with tomato Ketchup (see page 111).

Scalloped Potatoes

4	med. potatoes
1	small onion sliced
2	cups water
⅔	cup raw cashews
2	tbsp unbleached white flour
½	tsp salt

Serves 4

TIP

Sprinkle grated cheese over potatoes before baking.

1. Peel and slice potatoes into scallops and boil until slightly cooked. Drain and set aside.
2. Lightly sauté onion slices in a little olive oil.
3. Layer potato scallops and onion rings in the bottom of a vegetable oil-sprayed casserole dish.
4. Place water, cashews, flour and salt in a blender and blend until smooth. Pour blended mixture over potatoes.
5. Bake in a preheated oven at 350° for 30 to 45 minutes.

Pineapple Yams

2	med. whole yams
2	cups pineapple juice
2	tbsp cornstarch
½	tsp salt
1	14 oz can of pineapple rings
6	marachino cherries

Serves 4

1. Bake yams in skin until tender. Peel, slice and place in the bottom of vegetable oil-sprayed casserole dish.
2. In a small saucepan, dissolve cornstarch and salt in pineapple juice. Bring to a boil over medium heat, stirring constantly. Cook until mixture turns clear.
3. Pour the pineapple mixture evenly over the yams. Top with pineapple rings and garnish with marachino cherries.
4. Bake in a preheated oven at 350° for about 45 minutes.

Baked Squash

1		small hubbard squash
⅔	cup	raw cashews
½	cup	water
1	clove	fresh garlic minced
½	tsp	salt
½	tsp	seasoned salt
¾	cup	whole wheat bread crumbs

Serves 4

1. Peel squash and cut into ½" cubes. Place in pot, cover with water and simmer over low heat until tender. Drain water.
2. Place cashews and water in blender and blend until smooth and creamy.
3. Place cooked squash in bowl. Add seasoning and beat with electric beater until smooth. Pour in blended mixture and combine well.
4. Spoon squash into an oiled casserole dish and cover with bread crumbs.
5. Bake in a preheated oven at 325° for 20 minutes.

Parsnip and Carrot Balls

2	med.	carrots
3	med.	parsnips
½	cup	diced onions
½	cup	diced celery
½	cup	ground almonds
1	tsp	salt
1	cup	dry bread crumbs

Serves 4

1. Peel and slice carrots and parsnips. Place in pot, cover with water and boil until tender. Drain and set aside.
2. Lightly sauté onion and celery in a little olive oil.
3. In a large bowl, mash cooked carrots and parsnips. Add sautéed onions and celery, ground almonds, salt and half the bread crumbs.
4. Form mixture into small balls and role in remaining bread crumbs until evenly coated.
5. Arrange vegetable balls on a lightly oiled cookie sheet and bake at 375° for 30 minutes.

Zucchini Casserole

1	med. onion, diced	Serves 6
1	med. green pepper, diced	
1	small zucchini, chopped	
1½	cups cooked corn	
¼	tsp salt	
1½	cups Tomato Pasta Sauce (see page 77) or tomato soup	
¾	cup grated soy cheese	

1. Preheat oven to 350°.
2. In a non-stick or vegetable oil-sprayed fry pan, sauté onions, green pepper and zucchini until onions turn clear.
2. Add corn and salt to pan and cook until heated.
3. Place vegetables in a lightly oiled casserole dish. Pour tomato sauce or soup evenly over top and sprinkle with grated cheese.
4. Bake for 30 minutes or until cheese melts and casserole begins to bubble.

Festive Cauliflower

1	small cauliflower	Serves 4
2	med. carrots	
⅔	cup Melty Cheese Sauce (see page 101)	
	parsley	

1. Wash and core cauliflower. Put whole cauliflower in steamer and cook till tender.
2. While cauliflower is steaming, grate carrot on medium-sized grater. Stir fry carrots in a little olive oil until they turn bright orange.
3. Place cooked, whole cauliflower on a large platter. Spoon shredded carrot around cauliflower.
4. Cover cauliflower with Melty Cheese, sprinkle with parsley and serve.

Golden Carrots

2	cups	sliced, raw carrots	Serves 4
1	cup	water	
½	tsp	salt	
1	cup	canned undrained pineapple chunks	
3	tsp	cornstarch	
1	tsp	chopped parsley	

1. Place sliced carrots in pot. Add water and salt and cook until tender. Drain and reserve liquid.
2. Drain pineapple chunks and reserve juice.
3. Place carrot water, pineapple juice and cornstarch into a small sauce pan. Stir over medium heat until mixture thickens. Remove from heat.
4. Mix carrots and pineapple chunks together in a serving dish and pour sauce over them.
5. Sprinkle with chopped parsley and serve.

Salads, Salad Dressings & Cheeses

Four Bean Salad

1	cup	canned kidney beans, drained
1	cup	canned garbanzo beans, drained
1	cup	cooked green beans
1	cup	cooked yellow wax beans
½	cup	diced celery
1	small	onion, sliced in rings
½	large	green pepper, cut in strips
½	large	red pepper, cut in strips
⅔	cup	lemon juice
⅔	cup	honey

salt to taste

Serves 6

1. Drain and mix cold beans, celery, onion and pepper strips in a large bowl.
2. Blend lemon juice, honey and salt.
3. Pour over vegetables, cover and marinate in refrigerator overnight or for at least 6 hours.
4. Serve chilled with any entrée.

Cabbage Salad

1	small	cabbage diced fine
½	cup	diced celery
1	cup	shredded carrot
1	cup	crushed canned pineapple (optional)
½	cup	Tofu Mayonnaise (see page 96)

salt to taste

1. Mix diced cabbage, carrot, celery and pineapple together in a large bowl.
2. Add salt and Tofu Mayonnaise and combine well.
3. Chill and serve.

Serves 6

For a zesty flavor use Fresh Lemon and Garlic Dressing (see page 99) in the Cabbage Salad in place of the Tofu Mayonnaise.

Potato Salad

4	cups	cooked, diced potatoes	Serves 6
½	cup	finely diced celery	
½	cup	grated carrots	
¼	cup	cooked peas or corn	
¼	cup	diced cucumbers	
¼	cup	diced dill pickles	
¼	cup	diced green onions	
¼	cup	sliced radishes	
¾	cup	Tofu Mayonnaise (see page 96)	
1	tbsp	Low-Cal Mustard (see page 112)	

1 small tomato cut in wedges (optional)
salt and/or other seasonings to taste
green lettuce leaves
paprika

1. In a medium bowl, mix together potatoes, celery, carrots, peas/corn, cucumbers, dill pickles, green onions and radishes.
2. Add enough Tofu Mayonnaise and combine to evenly coat vegetables.
3. Add mustard, seasonings and salt to taste and mix well.
4. Line a large glass bowl with lettuce leaves and carefully spoon potato salad into bowl. Garnish edges of bowl with tomato wedges and sprinkle with paprika.
5. Chill and serve with burgers, baked beans or your favorite picnic lunch.

Cottage Cheese

1	lb	medium tofu drained
¼	tsp	garlic powder
¼	tsp	onion powder
½	tsp	lemon juice
1	tsp	salt
½	cup	raw cashews
¼	cup	pickle juice or water (reduce salt if using pickle juice)

Makes 2 cups

1. In a small bowl, rinse and crumble tofu.
2. Place remaining ingredients in blender and blend until smooth. Add just enough pickle juice or water to form a creamy sauce.
3. Pour blended sauce over crumbled tofu and mix well.
4. Chill and serve. Great served on baked potatoes, in lasagna or with rye bread.

Nettie's French Dressing

1	cup	water
⅓	cup	lemon juice
2 ½	tbsp	honey
2	tsp	paprika
1	tsp	celery salt
1	tsp	salad herbs
½	tsp	Italian seasoning
⅓	tsp	garlic powder
1	tsp	onion powder
1	tsp	salt

pinch of cayenne

1 ½	tbsp	*Cera Gel* or other powdered thickener that does not require heating
⅓	cup	olive oil

Makes 2 cups

1. Place all ingredients **except olive oil** in blender and blend briefly.
2. Add oil slowly and blend until creamy smooth.
3. Pour into serving jars and refrigerate. Serve chilled.

Lemon and Honey Dressing

1 cup freshly squeezed lemon juice
½ cup honey
1 tsp celery salt
¼ tsp garlic powder
½ tsp onion powder
⅛ tsp paprika
salt to taste
2½ tsp *Cera Gel* or other powdered thickener that does not require heating
1 tbsp your favorite fresh chopped herbs (optional)

Makes 2 cups

1. Place all ingredients except *Cera Gel* and chopped herbs in blender and blend briefly. Add *Cera Gel* and blend until thickened.
2. Stir in fresh chopped parsley, dill or other favorite herbs.
3. Pour into serving jars and refrigerate. Serve chilled.

Thousand Island Dressing

¼ recipe Tofu Mayonnaise (see page 96)
⅓ cup Ketchup (see page 111)
1 tsp paprika
1 tbsp finely diced green onions or chives
2 tbsp finely diced red and green peppers
1 tbsp finely diced sweet pickles

Makes 1 ½ cups

1. Place Tofu Mayonnaise, Ketchup and paprika in blender. Blend until combined.
2. Stir in diced vegetables.
3. Pour into serving jars and refrigerate overnight. Serve chilled as dressing or dip.

Gisele's Greek Salad

½ large   red onion
½ large   green pepper
3   roma tomatoes
½   long English cucumber
½ head   romaine lettuce (optional)
2 cloves   garlic
½   cup   garbanzo beans, drained
           (reserve juice for dressing)
12   Greek olives
1 recipe   Greek Salad Dressing
           (see page 99)

Serves 4

1. Rub the inside of a large wooden salad bowl with cut garlic cloves.
2. Chop onion, green pepper, tomatoes, cucumber and lettuce into large chunks and put in salad bowl. Mix together.
3. Add garbanzo beans and Greek olives.
4. Pour Greek Salad Dressing over all and toss well.
5. Serve immediately.

Tofu Mayonnaise

½   cup   raw cashews
⅓   cup   water
⅓   cup   lemon juice
1   lb   medium tofu, drained and
           rinsed
1   tsp   salt
1   tsp   onion powder
1   tbsp   honey
1   tbsp   fresh dill (optional)

Makes 3 cups

T**I**P

To dress up this basic mayonnaise, simply add ½ teaspoon of your favorite seasoning in the blender along with the other ingredients.

1. Place all ingredients in blender and blend until smooth and creamy. Do not underblend.
2. Pour into serving jars and refrigerate.
3. Serve chilled with your favorite salads or use as a dip for fresh vegetables.

Opposite Page

Fresh Lemon and Garlic Dressing

Makes 2 cups

½ cup   fresh lemon juice
½ cup   honey
1   clove   fresh garlic minced
¾ tsp   sea salt
⅛ cup   olive oil
1   cup   cold water
1   tbsp   *Cera Gel*
4   sprigs   fresh parsley, diced fine

1. Place all ingredients **except water, *Cera Gel* and parsley** in blender and blend until smooth and creamy.
2. Add cold water and blend for 1 minute.
3. Slowly add *Cera Gel*, 1 tablespoon at a time while continuing to blend.
4. Stir in fresh parsley. Pour into glass container and let chill for 30 minutes before serving.

Greek Salad Dressing

Makes 1 cup

¼ cup   juice from canned garbanzo beans
1   tbsp   olive oil
⅓ cup   lemon juice
2   tbsp   honey
salt and oregano to taste

1. Place bean juice, olive oil, lemon juice and honey in blender and blend until smooth.
2. Refrigerate 30 minutes or until well chilled.
3. Pour over Greek salad, toss and sprinkle with salt and oregano.

Opposite Page

Open Grilled Cheese or Grilled Garlic Toast (on buns)—page 117
Pita Pockets—page 122
Nachos—page 122

Jack Cheese

¼	cup	water
¼	cup	unflavored gelatin
¾	cup	boiling water
1	cup	raw cashews
¼	cup	nutritional yeast
1½	tsp	salt
1	tsp	onion powder
¼	tsp	garlic powder
¼	cup	lemon juice
2	tbsp	chopped red pepper
⅔	cup	soy cheese (optional)

Makes 3 cups

If you use soy cheese in this recipe, reduce the amount of nutritional yeast to 1 tablespoon.

1. Place gelatin and ¼ cup water in the blender and let soak for 5 minutes.
2. Pour boiling water over soaked gelatin and blend briefly to dissolve. Allow mixture to cool slightly.
3. Add cashews and blend until very smooth.
4. Add remaining ingredients and continue to blend until mixture is creamy.
5. Pour liquid into an oiled plastic container and let cool. Cover and refrigerate overnight.
6. Slice and serve with sliced breads, crackers, pickles and olives.

Melty Cheese

2	cups	water
4	oz	chopped pimento
2	tbsp	nutritional yeast
1½	tsp	salt
½	tsp	onion powder
¼	tsp	garlic powder
3	tbsp	cornstarch
1	cup	raw cashews
1½	tbsp	lemon juice
½	cup	soy cheese (optional)

Makes 3 cups

1. Place all ingredients in blender and blend until smooth and creamy.
2. Pour mixture in heavy saucepan and cook over medium heat 5 to 6 minutes, stirring constantly until thick.
3. Pour mixture into container or serve immediately.
4. Serve warm as a dip for corn chips or as a cheese sauce for vegetables.

Soy Cream Cheese

2	tbsp	unflavored gelatin
⅓	cup	water
½	cup	boiling water
1	cup	raw cashews
1	tbsp	salt
2	tbsp	lemon juice
1½	lb	medium tofu, drained and rinsed

Makes 3 cups

1. Place gelatin and ⅓ cup water in the blender and let soak for 5 minutes.
2. Pour ½ cup boiling water over soaked gelatin and blend briefly to dissolve. Allow mixture to cool slightly.
3. Add cashews and blend until very smooth.
4. Add remaining ingredients and continue blending until mixture is creamy.
5. Pour liquid into mold and refrigerate until set.
6. Garnish with olives and red or green peppers. Serve as a sandwich spread or on bagels.

Sauces & Gravies

Sauces & Gravies

By Phil Brewer

For most vegetarian cooks this is where the challenge really begins. Although anyone can steam and serve vegetables, very few of us enjoy eating just plain vegetables. Whenever we see mashed potatoes, we invariably look for the brown gravy. Steamed cauliflower and broccoli just taste better when served under a tangy cheese sauce. One of the most important principles in cooking is to satisfy the appetite. If the food eaten is not relished, then the body will not be as well nourished.

So, how do you make gravy without the bone, or the cheese sauce without the cheese? The answers are found in this section, which contains a few of our favorite Guest House sauce and gravy recipes. Many of our guests can't believe how gravies and sauces that are this delicious can possibly be made without using animal fat. Once you try them, you'll use them over and over.

Basic Cream Sauce

1	cup	raw cashews or blanched almonds
3	cups	water
2	tbsp	unbleached white flour
1	tsp	salt
1	tbsp	chicken style seasoning (optional)
½	tsp	onion powder (optional)
½	tsp	onion powder (optional)
½	tsp	celery salt (optional)

Makes 3 cups

Use a cream sauce to enrich soups, pastas, stroganoff and vegetables.

1. Place cashews or almonds into blender. Add 1 cup of water and blend until very smooth and creamy.
2. Add all remaining ingredients **except water** and continue blending.
3. In a saucepan, bring 2 cups of water to a boil.
4. Add blended mixture to boiling water and stir constantly while bringing to a second boil. Remove from heat.
5. Serve hot over vegetables or use as a sauce for Scalloped Potatoes (see page 86), creamed noodles or creamed soups. If you want to make a plain white sauce, simply omit the seasonings.

Chicken Gravy

2   cups water
½   cup   raw cashews
1   tbsp unbleached white flour
1   tbsp chicken style seasoning
2   tsp   onion powder
¼   tsp   celery salt
1   tsp   dill (optional)
salt to taste (optional)
1   tbsp soya sauce

Makes 2½ cups

1. Place all ingredients in blender and blend until smooth and creamy.
2. Pour blended mixture into small saucepan. Stir constantly over medium heat until thickened.
3. Serve hot over your favorite entrees.

Mary's Brown Gravy

½   cup   raw cashews
1   cup   water
2   cups water
⅓   cup   unbleached white flour
1   tsp   salt
1   tsp   chicken style seasoning
½   tsp   beef style seasoning
1   tsp   soy sauce
1   tbsp *Marmite* or other yeast extract seasoning
dash garlic salt

Makes 4 cups

T**I**P

Use this gravy to enrich stews, potatoes, patties and rice loaves.

1. Place cashews and 1 cup water into blender and blend until smooth.
2. Add remaining ingredients to blender and continue blending until creamy.
3. Pour mixture into small saucepan. Bring to a boil, stirring constantly (if too thick, add a little water).
4. Serve hot over your favorite entrees.

Tofu Sour Cream

1	lb	medium tofu, drained and rinsed	Makes 2 cups
½	cup	water	
1	tbsp	olive oil	
1	tsp	onion powder	
1	tsp	salt	
1	tsp	chicken style seasoning	

1. Place all ingredients in blender and blend until creamy smooth.
2. Chill in refrigerator for 1 hour.
3. Serve with baked potatoes.

Sweet & Sour Sauce

2	cups	pineapple juice	Makes 4 cups
½	cup	Ketchup (see page 111)	
2	tbsp	tomato paste	
2	tbsp	soy sauce (optional)	
1	tbsp	honey	
1	tbsp	lemon juice	
2	tbsp	cornstarch	
¼	cup	cold water	

salt to taste

1. In a small saucepan, combine pineapple juice, Ketchup, tomato paste, soy sauce, honey and lemon juice and bring to a boil.
2. Mix cornstarch in cold water and add to saucepan mixture, stirring constantly until thickened. Remove from heat.
3. Serve hot with Sweet & Sour Tofu (see page 71), Stir Fry Vegetables (see page 70) and Fried Rice (see page 71).

Cranberry Sauce

1	12	oz packagefrozen cranberries (do not thaw berries)	Makes 4 cups
1	large	apple, any variety	
½	cup	fresh orange pieces, including peel	
⅓	cup	melted honey or liquid honey	

1. Place frozen cranberries in blender, a few at a time, so they don't turn to mush as you blend them. Pour blended berries into serving bowl and set aside.
2. Place orange pieces in blender. Add melted or liquid honey and blend. Pour over cranberries and mix together.
3. Peel and grate apple. Add apple pieces to cranberry-orange mixture and stir.
4. Place cranberry sauce in fridge and let chill for 1 hour.
5. Serve with Bread Dressing (see page 60).

Tartar Sauce

½	cup	Tofu Mayonnaise	Makes 1 cup
⅓	cup	pickle relish	
1	tsp	prepared mustard	
1	tsp	minced parsley	

1. In a small bowl combine all ingredients and mix thoroughly.
2. Chill and serve with Fish Sticks (see page 64).

Corn Butter

2	tsp	unflavored gelatin
¼	cup	cold water
1	cup	boiling water
1	cup	unsalted cornmeal mush
¼	cup	raw cashews
1	tsp	salt
2	tsp	lemon juice
½	tsp	grated raw carrot (or enough to give color)

1. Place gelatin and ¼ cup cold water in blender and soak for 5 minutes.
2. Pour 1 cup boiling water into soaked gelatin and blend briefly to dissolve.
3. Place remaining ingredients in blender and blend thoroughly until smooth and creamy.
4. Pour into small serving jars and refrigerate until cool.
5. Serve as a bread spread or in place of margarine or butter.

Makes 2 cups

 TIP

Make cornmeal mush by placing ¼ cup cornmeal and ¾ cup water in a microwaveable dish and microwave on high for 3 minutes. Stir and microwave another 2 minutes.

Garlic Butter

¾	cup	warm, unsalted cornmeal mush
½	cup	raw cashews
½	cup	ground sesame seeds
3	cloves	garlic
1	tbsp	yeast flakes
1	tbsp	onion flakes
1	tsp	salt
4	tsp	lemon juice
1	cup	water

1. Place all ingredients into blender and blend about 2 minutes or until very smooth.
2. Pour into small serving jars and refrigerate.

Makes 2 cups

Guacamole

5	ripe	avocados
½	tsp	lemon juice
½	tsp	salt
1	tbsp	mild salsa (use spicier salsa for a more zesty flavor)

1. Peel and remove pits from avocados.
2. In a small bowl, mash avocados thoroughly. Add remaining ingredients and mix well together.
3. Serve with Spanish Rice (see page 75), tacos and nachos.

Makes 2 cups

To keep guacamole from turning brown, put avocado pits back in the guacamole bowl after mixing.

Aufstrich Paté

1	large	cooking onion, diced fine
1	tbsp	olive oil
⅓	cup	soy flour
1	cup	crushed cornflakes
1	cup	water
½	tsp	(or to taste) basil, summer savory, paprika, garlic and salt

1. Add olive oil to fry pan and sauté onions until tender.
2. Add flour, cornflake crumbs and water and simmer for 5 minutes. Mix in seasonings to your liking and allow to cool.
3. Place cooled mixture in blender and blend until smooth.
4. Chill and serve with rye bread slices, whole wheat crackers, dill pickles and olives.

Makes 3 cups

Flaxseed Gel

| 2 | cup | water |
| 6 | tbsp | flaxseeds |

¼ cup flaxseed
gel=1 egg

1. In small pot, add flaxseed and water and bring to a boil. Almost as soon as it begins to boil, it will turn from a watery liquid to a jelly-like consistency.
2. Remove from stove and immediately pour flaxseed mixture through a strainer and into a container.
3. Cool and store in refrigerator. Use as an egg white replacer and binding agent.

Step 2

Ketchup

4	cups	tomato juice
1	cup	honey
1	cup	lemon juice
⅛	tsp	cayenne pepper
¼	tsp	cinnamon
1	tsp	salt

Makes 4 cups

1. Place tomato juice, honey and lemon juice in a medium saucepan. Add seasonings and bring to a slow boil.
2. Simmer, uncovered, over low heat approximately 1½ hours or until sauce cooks down to about half the original amount.
3. Pour into jars and refrigerate.
4. When ready to use blend 1 cup of ketchup together with ¼ cup canned tomato paste.
5. Chill and serve.

Low-cal Mustard

2	tbsp	olive oil
1	tsp	turmeric
½	tsp	salt
¼	cup	unbleached white flour
½	cup	water
1	clove	garlic
⅓	cup	lemon juice

Makes 2 cups

1. Place olive oil, turmeric, salt and flour in blender. Add water and blend until smooth.
2. Put blended mixture in saucepan and cook until thickened.
3. Return sauce to blender and add garlic.
4. While blending, slowly add the lemon juice.
5. Pour into jars and refrigerate until chilled and thickened.
6. Use in Potato Salad (see page 93), as a spread on burgers and sandwiches.

Sandwiches & Fun Foods

Garlic Bread & Garlic Butter

½ cup   Corn Butter (see page 109)
2 ½ tbsp olive oil
1 ½ tsp   garlic powder
1   tsp   *Herbamare* or other salt sub-
          stitute
1   loaf whole wheat french bread, cut
          into slices

1. In a small bowl, mix together corn butter, olive oil, garlic powder and salt to make the garlic butter spread.
2. Spread one side of bread slices with garlic butter.
3. Assemble slices back into a loaf and wrap loaf in tin foil, leaving a little crack in the foil to let out moisture.
4. Bake at 350° for 30 minutes.
5. Serve immediately.

Serves 4 to 6

T💧P

For a toasty garlic bread, try toasting each slice on a heated skillet or fry pan instead of in the oven.

Cinnamon Toast

6   slices whole wheat bread
2   tbsp Corn Butter (see page 109)
3   tbsp brown sugar
½   tsp   cinnamon

1. Preheat oven to 350°.
2. Spread corn butter on bread.
3. Mix cinnamon and brown sugar together on a flat plate.
4. Dip buttered sides of bread into sugar mixture.
5. Place bread, sugared side up, onto cookie sheet and bake for 15 minutes or until nicely toasted.
6. Serve hot with Fruit Soup (see page 127).

Serves 4

Opposite Page

Open Grilled Cheese or Grilled Garlic Toast

Serves 4

6 slices whole wheat bread
1 recipe Jack Cheese (see page 100) or Garlic Butter (see page 109)
1 large tomato, sliced
1 green pepper, cut into rings
½ cup sliced olives

For variety use 6 burger style buns instead of bread slices.

1. Preheat oven to 325°.
2. Spread Jack Cheese or Garlic Butter over bread.
3. Cut tomato slices in half and place over spread.
4. Cover with pepper rings and sprinkle with olives.
5. Place on oven rack or cookie sheet and grill about 5 minutes or until cheese browns.
6. Serve with a hot soup.

Cashew Rice & Veggie Sandwiches

1½ cups crumbled Cashew Rice Loaf (see page 55)
½ cup Mayonnaise (see page 96)
¼ cup chopped pickles
⅓ cup mixed green and red peppers, chopped fine
½ cup diced celery
1 loaf whole grain bread cut lengthwise

Serves 4 to 6

Make cold sandwiches ahead of time, wrap tightly in plastic wrap and store in the fridge until ready to serve.

1. In a large bowl, combine cashew rice loaf, chopped pickles, peppers, celery and mayonnaise to make a spread.
2. Spread mixture evenly on each long bread slice.
3. Roll tightly lengthwise and cut into serving sizes.
4. Serve with fresh vegetables and dip.

Opposite Page

Banana Bread—page 27
Fruit Soup—page 127
Baked Apples—page 40

Ribbon Sandwiches

1 ½ cups ground Cashew Rice Loaf
          (see page 55)
⅓   cup   Mayonnaise (see page 96)
1   tbsp pickle juice
½   recipe Jack Cheese (see page 100)
½   recipe Cream Cheese (see page 101)
8   slices whole wheat bread

1. In a large bowl, crumble Cashew Rice
   Loaf. Add Tofu Mayonnaise and pickle
   juice to form a spread.
2. Remove crusts from bread. (Save and dry
   crusts to make bread crumbs.)
3. Spread one slice of bread with Cream
   Cheese, one slice with Jack Cheese and
   one slice with Cashew Rice Loaf mixture.
   Repeat on remaining bread slices.
4. Stack bread slices to form a layered sandwich. Cut diagonally into four or into 1"
   ribbons.
5. Serve with other party sandwiches, pickles, olives, and crackers and cheese.

Serves 4

Replace Cashew
Rice Loaf with a
commercial soy
chicken. Add
enough mayon-
naise to make it a
spreading
consistency.

Step 4

Party Sandwiches

1   loaf whole grain bread cut length-
          wise
½   cup   Soy Cream Cheese
          (see page 101)
½   cup   Manzanilla olives
Cherry tomatoes

1. Remove crust from bread and spread with
   Soy Cream Cheese.
2. Place a row of Manzanilla olives along one
   long end of the bread.
3. Roll tightly lengthwise and cut into serv-
   ing-sized slices.
4. Garnish with cherry tomatoes and serve
   with Ribbon Sandwiches (see page 118)
   and Mocktails (see page 123).

Serves 4 to 6

Replace Manza-
nilla olives with
red and green
maraschino cher-
ries to make fes-
tive Christmas
party sandwiches.

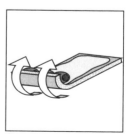

Step 3

Grilled Cheese Sandwiches

6 slices whole wheat bread
1 recipe Jack Cheese (see page 100) or
   commercial soy cheese
2 tbsp Corn Butter (see page 109)
Slices of your favourite vegetables
   (onion, tomato, green pepper)

Serves 4

1. Spray grill or fry pan with vegetable oil
   and preheat to medium heat.
2. Spread corn butter on one side of each
   piece of bread.
3. Spread cheese and place vegetable slices
   on unbuttered side of bread.
4. Place sandwich, buttered side down, on
   grill and cook until golden brown. Turn
   sandwich over and brown the other side.
   Make sure cheese melts.

French Bread Pizza

1 loaf whole wheat french bread, cut
    lengthwise
¾ cup tomato sauce (your own or
    commercial brand)
1 cup sliced black olives
1   green pepper, cut into rings
1 cup unsweetened, canned
    pineapple chunks
1½ cups crumbled soy cheese or Jack
    Cheese (see page 100)

Serves 4

1. Preheat oven to 350°.
2. Spread french bread slices with tomato
   sauce and add all or any of the above toppings. Sprinkle with cheese.
3. Bake on a lightly oiled cookie sheet for 10
   to 15 minutes.
4. Cut and serve hot with a salad.

Yummy Crackers

1¾	cups	ground oat flakes	Serves 4
½	cup	ground almonds	
½	cup	unbleached white flour	
¼	cup	whole wheat flour	
½	cup	fine ground coconut	
½	cup	water	
1	tbsp	honey	
1	tbsp	peanut butter	
½	tsp	vanilla	
1	tsp	salt	

1. In a large bowl, combine oat flakes, almonds, white and whole wheat flour.
2. Place remaining ingredients in blender and blend until creamy.
3. Add blended mixture to dry ingredients and mix thoroughly.
4. Place dough onto a lightly floured surface and roll out until very thin (¹⁄₁₆").
5. Use cookie cutters or a jar lid to cut dough into rings, shapes or squares.
6. Use a spatula to lift the crackers onto a vegetable oil-sprayed cookie sheet.
7. Bake approximately 10 minutes at 400° or until golden brown.

Popcorn

½	cup	popcorn kernels	Serves 4
2	tbsp	olive oil (or to taste)	
1	tbsp	*Herbamare* or other salt substitute (or to taste)	

1. Pop desired amount of popcorn in a hot air corn popper. Place popcorn in a large bowl or pot.
2. Sprinkle with olive oil and salt and toss well.

Crackerjacks

4	cups	freshly popped corn	Serves 4
½	cup	coarsely chopped nuts (walnuts, almonds, pecans)	
⅛	cup	honey	
½	tbsp	molasses	
1	tsp	vanilla	

1. Go through the popcorn and remove all unpopped kernels. Then place popcorn in a large bowl and add in chopped nuts.
2. In a small pot slowly heat honey, molasses and vanilla until mixture is smooth.
3. Pour hot liquid over popcorn, stirring constantly, until popcorn and nuts are well coated.
4. Spread glazed popcorn evenly on an ungreased cookie sheet.
5. Bake 10 to 15 minutes at 325° or until golden. Turn popcorn often and watch carefully while baking as it burns easily.
6. Let mixture cool on cookie sheet. Store in an airtight container until ready to serve.

Nachos

1	pkg	Corn chips
6	oz	shredded soy cheese
1	cup	diced green peppers, tomatoes and black olives
1	cup	salsa (your own or commercial brand)
1	cup	Guacamole (see page 110)

1. Preheat oven to 350°.
2. Cover 4 oven-safe plates with tin foil.
3. On each plate, place a couple of layers of corn chips and cheese and bake for 5 minutes or until cheese is melted.
4. Sprinkle hot corn chips with diced peppers, tomato and olives.
5. Serve with salsa and Guacamole.

Serves 4

 P

Placing tin foil on the plates keeps the cheese from baking onto them.

 P

Bake corn chips without the cheese and serve Melty Cheese (see page 101) as a side dip instead.

Pita Pockets

4		whole wheat pita bread shells
¼	cup	Tofu Mayonnaise (see page 96)
1	cup	shredded lettuce
1	cup	diced tomatoes
1	cup	alfalfa sprouts (optional)
1	cup	mild salsa (your own or commercial brand)
1	cup	Guacamole (see page 110)
½	cup	shredded soy cheese

1. Cut pita bread shells in half. Open up and layer with any or all of the above ingredients.
2. Serve with nachos or soup.

Serves 4

Tropical Mocktail

⅛ cup   orange grenadine syrup
⅛ cup   lime grenadine syrup
¼ cup   orange juice concentrate
½ cup   ice
carbonated water

Makes 1 12-ounce glass

1. Place orange and lime syrup, orange juice and ice into blender and blend until ice is smooth.
2. Pour liquid into a 12-ounce glass and top up with carbonated water.
3. Garnish with a lime slice and serve immediately.

Strawberry Mocktail

¼ cup   strawberry grenadine syrup
⅓ cup   frozen strawberries
½ cup   ice
carbonated water

Makes 1 12-ounce glass

1. Place strawberry syrup, strawberries and ice into blender and blend until ice is smooth.
2. Pour liquid into a 12-ounce glass and top up with carbonated water.
3. Garnish with a lime slice and serve immediately.

Soups

Chicken Noodle Soup

1	tsp	olive oil	Serves 4
½	cup	chopped onions	
½	cup	chopped celery	
½	cup	shredded carrot	
6	cups	water	
⅓	cup	chicken style seasoning	
¼	tsp	celery salt	

salt to taste
dash of cayenne (optional)

| 3 | cups | precooked and rinsed pasta noodles |

1. In the bottom of a large pot sauté onions with olive oil.
2. Add celery and carrots, stir and cook for a minute.
3. Add water and seasonings and bring to a full boil.
4. Reduce heat and add noodles. Simmer for 15 minutes.

Split Pea Chowder

3	cups	water	Serves 4
¼	cup	brown rice	
1	cup	split peas	
1	tsp	salt	
½	cup	sautéed onions	
¼	cup	finely diced carrots	
¼	cup	finely diced celery	
¼	tsp	basil	

1. Pour water into a 2-quart saucepan and bring to a boil.
2. Add rice to rapidly boiling water. Cover, reduce heat and let cook 30 minutes.
3. Add split peas and cook another 30 minutes.
4. Add remaining ingredients, stir and let simmer 10 to 12 minutes or until vegetables are tender.
5. Serve hot with croutons and Garlic Toast (see page 117).

Corn Chowder

6	cups	water
½	cup	diced onion
1	tbsp	olive oil
½	cup	chicken style seasoning
1	tsp	salt
1	tbsp	diced parsley (fresh or dried)
½	tsp	onion powder
½	tsp	celery salt

dash cayenne (optional)

1½	cups	diced potatoes
⅓	cup	grated carrots
⅓	cup	diced celery
1½	cups	corn (frozen or canned)
1	cup	raw cashews
1	cup	water

Serves 4 to 6

1. Sauté onion in olive oil in bottom of a large saucepan until clear.
2. Add water and bring to a boil. Add seasoning and vegetables except corn. Simmer until soft. Add corn.
3. Blend cashews in 1 cup of water until creamy and smooth. Slowly add to soup and bring to a slow boil.
4. Serve immediately with Cheese Biscuits (see page 30).

Fruit Soup

3	cups	apple juice
½	cup	orange or raspberry juice concentrate
1	cup	dried and cut up fruit pieces (pears, apricots, prunes, etc.)
⅓	cup	honey
2	tbsp	cornstarch
1 10 oz		can of undrained peaches

Serves 4 to 6

1. In a large pot, pour in apple juice and fruit juice concentrate and bring to a boil.
2. Add dried fruit and honey and continue boiling.
3. Mix cornstarch in a little water and add to boiling mixture. Cook for 5 minutes.
4. Add canned fruit and stir.
5. Serve hot or cold.

Cream of Cauliflower Soup

1	tbsp	olive oil	Serves 6
1	cup	diced onions	
6	cups	water	
2	tsp	salt	
½	cup	chicken style seasoning	
1	tsp	onion powder	
¼	tsp	garlic powder	
1	tbsp	dried parsley	
1	cup	diced celery	
2	cups	diced potatoes	
⅔	cup	shredded carrots	
1	cup	raw cashews	
4	cups	water	
1½	cups	chopped, fresh cauliflower	
1	cup	frozen or fresh peas	

1. In a large 4-quart pot, sauté onions in olive oil until clear.
2. Pour in 6 cups of water, add seasonings and bring to a boil.
3. Add celery, potatoes and carrots, and simmer over low heat until cooked.
4. Place cashews and 2 cups water in a blender and blend until creamy and smooth.
5. Add blended mixture to soup stock and bring to a boil, stirring constantly. Reduce heat.
6. Add fresh cauliflower and peas 5 minutes before serving.

Cream of Fresh Vegetable Soup

1½ cups	chopped, fresh vegetable (e.g. peas, broccoli, asparagus)	Serves 6
1	tbsp	olive oil
½	cup	diced onion
¼	cup	diced celery
⅛	cup	shredded carrot
⅔	cup	diced fresh vegetables (same as selected above)
4	cups	water
⅔	cup	raw cashews
2	tbsp	chicken style seasoning
1	tsp	salt
½	tsp	onion powder
¼	tsp	celery salt

1. Steam 1½ cups vegetables in a small amount of water until cooked.
2. Placed steamed vegetables in blender and blend until smooth. Place blended vegetables in a small bowl.
3. Pour olive oil in the bottom of a 2-quart saucepan and sauté onion, celery and carrot.
4. Add 3 cups of water to saucepan and bring to a slow boil. Add blended vegetables and ⅔ cup of chopped fresh vegetables. Simmer for 5 minutes.
5. Place cashews, 1 cup of water and seasonings in blender and blend until smooth and creamy. Slowly add to soup and bring to a boil. Serve.

Russian Borscht

Part 1   Serves 4

    2   cups water
    1   med. potatoes, peeled and cubed
    1   large carrot, peeled and diced
    1   small beet, peeled and cubed
    1   small onion, chopped
    1   tsp   salt

1. In a two quart saucepan bring water to boil. Add vegetables and simmer until tender.
2. Drain water. Place cooked vegetables and salt in blender and blend until smooth. Set aside.

Part 2

    ½   cup   chopped onion
    1   tbsp olive oil
    2   cups canned whole tomatoes, drained and chopped
    ½   cup   shredded carrots
    ¼   cup   diced beets
    ¼   cup   diced celery
    ¼   cup   canned corn (optional)
    ½   cup   diced raw potatoes
    3   cups canned tomatoes
    1   cup   cooked shredded cabbage
    1   tsp   dill
    1   tsp   garlic salt
    1   cup   water
    ½   cup   raw cashews

1. In a 3-quart saucepan, sauté onions in olive oil until clear. Add water and seasonings and bring to a boil.
2. Add all vegetables to boiling water and simmer until tender.
3. Add blended vegetables from Part 1 and continue simmering for 5 minutes.
4. Blend cashews with 1 cup water until creamy and smooth. Add slowly to soup and simmer for 5 minutes.
5. Garnish with fresh diced parsley and serve.

Tomato Soup

6	cups	tomato juice
¼	cup	unbleached white flour
½	tsp	celery salt
1	tsp	onion powder
¼	tsp	garlic powder (optional)
1	tbsp	maple syrup

salt to taste
dash cayenne (optional)

Serves 6

1. In a 4-quart sauce pan, bring 5 cups of tomato juice to a boil.
2. Place remaining 1 cup of tomato juice, flour and seasonings in the blender and blend until smooth.
3. Add blended mixture to boiling tomato juice. Stir until clear.
4. Serve with Bread Sticks (see page 30).

Tomato Vegetable Soup

1	tbsp	olive oil
1	med.	onion, diced fine
6	cups	water
1		bay leaf
⅓	cup	chicken style seasoning
1	tbsp	dried parsley
1	tsp	garlic salt
1	tsp	salt
¼	cup	pearl barley
2	med.	potatoes, diced fine
2		carrots, grated
2		stalks celery, diced fine
2	cups	tomato juice

Serves 6

For variety, replace pearl barley with ½ cup alphabets pasta in Tomato Vegetable Soup.

1. In a large pot, sauté onions in olive oil until onions cook clear. Add water and bring to a boil.
2. Add seasonings and barley. Reduce heat, cover and allow to boil slowly for 20 minutes.
3. Add vegetables, cover and let simmer for 5 minutes.
4. Add tomato juice, cover and let simmer for 10 minutes.
5. Serve hot with Grilled Cheese Sandwiches (see page 119).

Opposite Page

Italian Bread Sticks—page 30
Cream of Cauliflower Soup—page 128
Tomato Vegetable Soup—page 131
Pizza—page 119

Following Page

Trifle—page 156
Pumpkin Squares—page 141
Pineapple Cheesecake—page 139

Desserts

Sugar, Sugar, Sugar

By Phil Brewer

Sugar in the morning, sugar in the evening, and sugar at supper time. It takes about 90 feet of sugar cane to produce the 36 teaspoons of sugar every man, woman and child in North America consumes on average each day. Because commercial food processing contributes nearly 70% of the sugar we eat, most people find it hard to believe they are eating that much sugar each day. If you examine the labels, you'll find that sugar is a major ingredient in most commercial foods from peanut butter to salad dressings to ketchup. Even brand name breakfast cereals contain about 20% sugar.

It is not hard for health conscious individuals to be horrified with this "sugar addiction" and go to the other extreme of eliminating all sugars from their diet. However, Eileen decided she didn't want our children to feel that they were somehow deprived because they were not eating refined sugar products. She ensured that our meals included desserts, special treats and holiday favorites that were just as delicious, but made with considerably less amounts of sugar. Our three children, who are now grown, have never had a cavity or suffered a toothache, but they have enjoyed a variety of "sweet" foods including brownies, fudge, cookies and ice cream. It is possible to enjoy your desserts and still maintain a healthy body.

Basic White Cake

1	cup	raw cashews
⅔	cup	water
½	cup	honey
½	tsp	salt
1	tsp	vanilla
2	tsp	*egg replacer* or commercial egg replacement product
1	tsp	lemon juice
1	cup	unbleached white flour
2½	tsp	baking powder

This basic cake recipe can be used to make a variety of delicious desserts. Makes one 8" x 8" cake

1. Preheat oven to 350°.
2. Place cashews and water into blender and blend until very smooth.
3. Add honey, salt, vanilla, *egg replacer* and lemon juice and blend again.
4. Pour blended ingredients into a large mixing bowl. Add flour and baking powder and mix until well combined.
5. Pour batter into a 8" x 8" cake pan that has been lightly sprayed with vegetable oil. Bake for 35 to 40 minutes or until done.
6. Remove from oven and allow to cool. Frost or decorate as desired and serve.

Apple Cake

1. Follow the first four steps of the Basic White Cake recipe. Pour batter into an 8" spring pan that has been sprayed with oil.
2. Peel, quarter and core two large apples. Cut part way through the top of each apple quarter so that it fans out. Place the apple fans evenly across the top of the batter.
3. Bake for 35 to 40 minutes or until an inserted toothpick comes out dry.
4. Cool and spinkle with icing sugar and serve.

Step 2

Flan Cake

1. Follow the first four steps of the basic cake recipe.
2. Pour batter into a flan pan that has been sprayed with oil and bake for 35 to 40 minutes or until an inserted toothpick comes out dry.
3. When cooled, spoon on one recipe of Vanilla Pudding (see page 156). Decorate with fresh fruit, glaze and serve.

Lemon Pecan Cake

1	cup	raw cashews	Makes an 8" cake
½	cup	honey	
2	tsp	*egg replacer* or commericial egg replacement product	
1	tsp	lemon flavoring	
¼	tsp	salt	
1	cup	cold water	
2	tsp	baking powder	
1	cup	unbleached white flour	
½	cup	chopped pecans	
¼	cup	brown sugar	
1	tbsp	finely grated lemon peel	
¼	cup	maple syrup	

1. Blend first six ingredients in blender until smooth.
2. Pour blended mixture into a large bowl and add flour and baking powder. Mix well.
3. In a small bowl, mix together brown sugar, pecans and lemon peel.
4. Pour maple syrup into the bottom of an oiled 8" x 8" cake pan.
5. Sprinkle pecan mixture over maple syrup. Then spoon cake batter on top of pecans. Bake at 350° for 30 minutes or until lightly browned.
5. Turn cake out of pan and let cool. Serve with Pear Ice Cream (see page 158) or fresh raspberries.

Pineapple Cheesecake

2	tbsp	unflavoured vegetable gelatin
¾	cup	pineapple juice
1	cup	boiling pineapple juice
⅓	cup	honey
1	cup	raw cashews
¼	cup	fine coconut (optional)
½	tsp	salt
6		ice cubes

1 10 oz can crushed pineapple (drained)

1. Place gelatin and ¾ cup pineapple juice in a blender and let soak for 10 minutes.
2. Pour 1 cup boiling pineapple juice over the soaked mixture and blend briefly to dissolve gelatin.
3. Add honey, cashews, coconut and salt to blender and blend until creamy.
4. Add ice cubes to the blender until the mixture reaches the 1 quart mark. Blend until smooth.
5. Pour blended mixture into a bowl and gently fold in crushed pineapple.
6. Pour over your favorite baked crumb crust or into parfait glasses.
7. Let stand until set and serve with a fruit topping.

Covers an 8" x 12" cake pan or fills 8 parfait glasses

T▽P

To make different flavors of cheesecakes, simply replace the pineapple juice and crushed pineapple with other fruit juice concentrates.

Kathy's Lemon Cheesecake

1	cup	water
¼	cup	unbleached white flour
¼	cup	honey
½	tsp	lemon extract
⅛	tsp	salt
2	tbsp	olive oil
2	tbsp	tofu milk powder
⅛	cup	water
2	tsp	vanilla
1	6 oz	package dessert tofu
¼	cup	lemon flavoured gelatin powder
1	tbsp	unflavoured gelatin

Fills one 8" pie crust shell or covers an 8" square cake pan

1. Place water, flour, honey, lemon extract and salt into a blender and blend until smooth.
2. Pour blended mixture into a small saucepan. Stir constantly over a medium heat until sauce comes to a slow boil.
3. Return mixture to blender and add all remaining ingredients. Blend until thick and creamy.
4. Pour sauce into a baked pie crust shell or over your favorite crumb crust.
5. Chill and serve.

Pumpkin Squares

2	tbsp	unflavoured gelatin
¾	cup	water
1	cup	boiling water
¾	cup	brown sugar or maple syrup
1	cup	raw cashews
2	tsp	cinnamon
½	tsp	salt
6		ice cubes
2	cups	cooked pumpkin

Covers an 8" x 12" pan

1. Place gelatin and ¾ cup water in a blender and soak for 1 minute.
2. Pour 1 cup boiling water over soaked mixture and blend briefly to dissolve gelatin.
3. Add brown sugar, cashews, cinnamon and salt to blender and liquify until creamy.
4. Add ice cubes to the blender until the mixture reaches the 1 quart mark. Blend until smooth.
5. Add pumpkin and blend until smooth.
6. Pour blended mixture over your favorite baked crumb crust.
7. Let stand until set, cut into squares and serve.

Grandma Smith's Pastry

⅔ cup   raw cashews
½ cup   warm water
1 tbsp yeast
1 tbsp liquid lecithin
1 cup   oat flour or 1 cup of quick oats
          blended very fine
1 cup   unbleached white flour
¼ tsp   salt

1. Place warm water, cashews and lecithin into blender and blend until smooth.
2. Pour blended mixture into a small bowl and stir in yeast. Let rise for 5 minutes.
3. In a large bowl, mix together oat flour, unbleached white flour and salt. Pour in blended mixture and stir until dough forms.
4. Knead lightly. Divide dough into two pieces and roll each piece on a floured surface until it fits an 8" pie pan.
5. Place one dough piece in the bottom of an oiled pie pan and fill with your favorite precooked filling. Place second piece on top and trim edges.
6. Bake at 350° for 35 minutes or until golden brown.

Makes one 8" pie crust top and bottom

Grandma Smith's pie pastry also makes an excellent pastry for tarts.

Use a pre-cooked filling as this type of crust bakes faster than a raw filling would require.

Crumb Pastry

1 cup   graham wafer crumbs
½ cup   unbleached white flour
⅓ cup   maple syrup

1. Preheat oven to 350°.
2. Mix graham crumbs and flour together in a small bowl.
3. Slowly cut maple syrup into the dry ingredients until the mixture just holds together when compressed.
4. Pat crumb mixture evenly over the bottom of a lightly oiled, 8" pie plate or 8" x 8" cake pan.
5. Bake for 10 minutes or until golden brown.
6. Cool and use with your favorite crumb pie recipes.

Makes one 8" pie crust

Coconut Pie Crust

1½ cups coconut (medium or fine)
1   tbsp unbleached white flour
¼   cup tofu milk

Makes one 8" pie crust

1. Preheat oven to 350°.
2. Mix coconut and flour together in a small bowl. Pour in milk and mix.
3. Pat crumb mixture evenly over the bottom of a lightly oiled, 8" pie plate or 8" x 8" cake pan.
4. Bake for 10 minutes or until the edges just begin to turn golden brown.
5. Cool and add cream filling.

Nettie's Coconut Cream Pie

3   cups hot water
¾   cup dried pineapple pieces
⅓   cup tofu milk powder
½   cup cornstarch
⅓   tsp salt
½   tsp vanilla
½   tsp coconut flavouring

Makes one 8" pie

TIP

To make a vanilla pie filling, simply omit the coconut flavoring.

1. Place hot water, pineapple, tofu milk powder, cornstarch and salt in a blender and blend until smooth.
2. Pour blended mixture into a saucepan. Stir constantly over a medium heat until sauce thickens.
3. Remove from heat and stir in vanilla and coconut flavouring.
4. Pour into a Coconut Pie Crust (see page 143) or other pre-baked pie crust.
5. Chill and serve.

Apple Pie

6		large cooking apples, peeled, cored and sliced	Makes one 8" pie
½	cup	water	
½	cup	brown sugar or maple syrup	
1	tsp	cinnamon (optional)	
1	tsp	fresh lemon juice	
½	tsp	vanilla	

1. Prepare one recipe Grandma Smith's Pastry (see page 142). Do not bake crusts.
2. Place apples and water in a saucepan. Cook over medium heat until apple slices are tender. Do not overcook the fruit.
3. Remove from heat. Add brown sugar, cinnamon, lemon juice and vanilla. Stir until ingredients are well mixed.
4. Lightly spray an 8" pie pan with vegetable oil. Place one pie crust on bottom, trim edges and pour apple filling over unbaked pie crust. Place the second pie crust on top. Pinch the edges of the two pie crusts together and cut off any excess crust.
5. Use a sharp knife to make 3 or 4 small incisions in the center of the top crust.
6. Bake in a preheated 350° oven for about 30 minutes or until top crust turns golden brown.
7. Serve warm with vanilla flavored Pear Ice Cream (see page 158).

Blueberry Pie

1	cup	frozen grape juice concentrate, undiluted
¼	cup	minute tapioca
3	cups	fresh, rinsed and drained blueberries or 1 package (20 oz) thawed, unsweetened blueberries
1½	tsp	vanilla
1½	tsp	lemon juice
pinch of salt		

Makes one 8" pie

1. Mix grape juice concentrate and tapioca together in a small saucepan and let stand 5 minutes.
2. Bring liquid to a boil, reduce heat and allow to simmer for about 5 minutes, stirring often.
3. Stir in blueberries, vanilla and lemon juice and let simmer another 5 minutes or until tapioca is clear.
4. Remove from heat and pour into baked pie shell.
5. Chill until firm and serve.

Carob Pie

2	cups	water
⅔	cup	raw cashews
1	tsp	vanilla
¼	tsp	salt
⅔	cup	maple syrup
3	tbsp	cornstarch
3	tbsp	carob powder
1	tbsp	*Caf Lib* or instant coffee substitute
⅓	cup	carob chips

Makes one 8" pie

TIP

To add a special touch, spread a layer of sliced bananas across the bottom of the pie crust before pouring the carob pie filling into pie shell.

1. Place all ingredients **except carob chips** in a blender and blend until creamy smooth.
2. Pour blended mixture into a small saucepan. Stir constantly over a medium heat until sauce comes to a slow boil.
3. Remove pot from heat and add carob chips. Stir until the carob chips are completely melted.
4. Pour mixture into prepared pie crust shell. Chill and serve.

Lemon Pie

3   cups   pineapple juice
½   cup   honey
½   cup   lemon flavoured gelatin
4   tbsp   cornstarch
pinch of salt
2   tbsp   fresh lemon juice
1   tsp   grated lemon rind (optional)

Fills one 8" pie
crust shell or a
dozen tart shells

1. Place pineapple juice, honey, lemon gelatin, cornstarch and salt in the blender and
   blend briefly.
2. Pour mixture into a saucepan. Stir and
   simmer over a low heat until it cooks
   clear.
3. Remove from heat and stir in lemon juice
   and grated lemon rind.
4. Pour into baked pie crusts or tart shells,
   chill and serve.

Basic Cookie Recipe

1	cup	raw cashews
⅔	cup	water
½	cup	brown sugar
2	tsp	*Egg Replacer* or other commercial egg replacement product
1	tsp	vanilla
1	tbsp	lemon juice
¾	tsp	salt
1	cup	unbleached white flour
2	tsp	baking powder
⅔	cup	raisins or carob chips
½	cup	chopped walnuts

This recipe can be used as the basis for a variety of different kinds of cookies. Makes 18 large cookies.

1. Place first seven ingredients into a blender and blend until smooth.
2. Pour blended mixture into a large mixing bowl. Add flour and baking powder and mix thoroughly.
3. Stir in raisins or carob chips and walnuts. Drop by spoonfuls onto an oiled cookie sheet.
4. Bake in a preheated 350° oven for about 20 minutes or until golden brown,
5. Remove from cookie sheet and allow to cool.

Basic Cookie Recipe Variations

Oatmeal cookies: Replace 1 cup flour with ½ cup of quick oats and ½ cup of flour.

Cinnamon raisin cookies: Add 1 teaspoon of cinnamon (or another favorite spice) to the recipe.

Pineapple cookies: Replace ⅔ cup of raisins with ⅔ cup of dried pineapple pieces (or dried papaya or dried apricot).

Here are a few of the varieties of cookies you can make with the basic cookie recipe. Don't be afraid to experiment.

Ilse's Honey Cookies

1	cup	commercial cashew or almond butter
⅔	cup	honey
2	tsp	*Egg Replacer* or other commercial egg replacement product in ¼ cup of water
2	tsp	baking powder
1	tsp	cinnamon
2	cups	finely chopped almonds
1½ cups		unbleached white flour

1. Preheat oven to 325°.
2. In a large bowl, mix together all ingredients **except the flour.**
3. Add flour, a bit at a time, until a soft dough forms. Place dough between two sheets of plastic wrap and roll it into a sheet about ¼" thick.
4. Remove the top sheet of plastic wrap and cut the dough into 1" squares. Use a spatula to lift the squares off of the bottom wrap and place them onto an oiled cookie sheet.
5. Bake for 10 to 12 minutes or until golden.
6. Remove from cookie sheet and allow to cool.

Makes 24 cookies

P

To make thimble cookies, roll the dough into small 1" balls. Press a hole in the center of each ball with your thumb. Fill the holes with your favorite jam and bake as directed.

Sesame Fingers

1½	cups	raw sesame seeds
¾	cups	fine, unsweetened coconut
½	cup	peanut butter
¼	cup	honey
¼	cup	brown sugar
1	tsp	vanilla
½	tsp	salt
½	cup	finely chopped walnuts or pecans

Makes 12 squares

1. Preheat oven to 300°.
2. In a large bowl, mix all ingredients together until a thick batter forms.
3. Press the batter, about ½" thick, across the bottom of a well-oiled or sprayed 9" x 12" baking pan.
4. Bake for about 30 minutes or until nicely browned.
5. Use a sharp knife to slice into finger shapes about 3" long. Separate slightly as fingers tend to stick together as they cool.
6. Serve or freeze and thaw as required.

Brownies

1	cup	raw cashews
⅔	cup	water
½	cup	brown sugar
⅓	cup	carob powder
1	tbsp	*Caf Lib* or other instant coffee substitute
½	tsp	salt
1	tsp	vanilla
2	tsp	*Egg Replacer* or commercial egg replacement product
1	tsp	lemon juice
1½	cups	unbleached white flour
2½	tsp	baking powder
½	cup	chopped walnuts

Makes one 8" square pan

T**▼**P

Make frosting by melting 1½ cup carob chips in the microwave for 1 minute. Spread over cake and sprinkle with ground walnuts.

1. Preheat oven to 350°.
2. Place cashews and water into blender and blend until very smooth.
3. Add brown sugar, carob powder, *Caf Lib*, salt, vanilla, *Egg Replacer* and lemon juice and blend again.
4. Pour blended ingredients into a large mixing bowl. Add flour, baking powder and walnuts and mix until well combined.
5. Pour batter into a 8" x 8" cake pan that has been lightly sprayed with vegetable oil. Bake for 35 to 40 minutes or until done.
6. Remove from oven and allow to cool. Frost or decorate as desired and serve.

Carob Fudge

1	cup	dates
1½	cups	carob chips
1	cup	peanut butter
½	cup	maple syrup
1	cup	chopped walnuts

Makes one 8" x 8" pan

1. Place carob chips in a large bowl and melt in microwave (or in a double boiler).
2. Add peanut butter, maple syrup and walnuts and mix until thoroughly combined.
3. Pat batter into a lightly oiled 8" x 8" pan. Chill.
4. Cut into squares and serve.

Carob Clusters

1	cup	carob chips
⅓	cup	peanut butter
½	cup	chopped walnuts or pecans

Makes 12 medium sized clusters

 TIP

1. Place carob chips and peanut butter in a small bowl and melt in microwave (or in a double boiler). Stir until evenly combined.
2. Stir in nuts and quickly drop by teaspoonfuls onto waxed paper.
3. Let set until hard. Store in refrigerator.

For a different taste, replace nuts with ½ cup raisins or ½ cup rice crispies.

Carob Kisses

1	cup	peanut butter
1	cup	chopped dates
½	cup	soft honey
1	cup	chopped walnuts or pecans
1	cup	ground granola
½	cup	tofu milk powder
2	tsp	lemon juice
3	cups	carob chips

Makes about 24 kisses

Step 3

1. In a large bowl thoroughly mix together all ingredients **except carob chips.** Roll batter into small balls.
2. Place carob chips in a small bowl and melt in microwave (or in a double boiler).
3. Quickly dip each ball into the melted carob and place on waxed paper.
4. Let set until hard. Store in refrigerator.

Carob Marshmallow Roll

1	cup	carob chips
2	tbsp	peanut butter
¼	cup	Flaxseed Gel (see page 111)
2	cups	miniature marshmallows
½	cup	chopped walnuts
¼	cup	shredded coconut

Serves 6 to 8

1. Place carob chips and peanut butter in a heavy saucepan. Melt and stir together over low heat.
2. Remove from heat and add Flax Seed Gel, marshmallows and walnuts. Stir until well combined.
3. Place mixture on one end of a sheet of wax paper covered with coconut and roll up.
4. Refrigerate or freeze.
5. Cut into slices and serve.

Festive Cornflake Squares

6	cups	corn flakes or other flake cereal
1	cup	chopped dried apricot
1	cup	chopped dried cranberries
1	cup	whole roasted almonds
4	cups	marshmallows

Makes 12 squares

TIP

Using an oiled spoon helps prevent sticking and makes mixing easier.

1. Combine cornflakes, apricots, cranberries and almonds in a large bowl.
2. Place marshmallows in a small bowl and microwave on high (about 3 minutes) to melt.
3. Pour melted marshmallows over cornflake mixture and stir until everything is well combined.
4. Press mixture into an oiled 8" x 12" pan and chill.
5. Cut into squares and serve.

Blueberry Kuchen

2	cups	unbleached white flour
¾	tsp	salt
½	cup	brown sugar
1	tsp	baking powder
⅔	cup	raw cashews
½	cup	water
1	tbsp	olive oil
2	cups	frozen or fresh unsweetened blueberries

Serves 6

TP

Substitute blueberries with fresh sweetened raspberries or pitted cherries.

1. Preheat over to 350°.
2. In a large bowl, combine flour, salt, brown sugar and baking powder.
3. Place cashews, water and oil in blender and blend until creamy and smooth.
4. Pour blended cashew butter over dry ingredients and mix gently until mixture sticks together when compressed.
5. Press 2/3 of the crumb mixture over the bottom of an oiled 8" x 8" baking pan.
6. Cover crust with blueberries. Sprinkle remaining 1/3 of the crumb mixture over the blueberries.
7. Bake for 30 minutes or until golden brown.
8. Serve warm or cold with Pear Ice Cream (see page 158) or a non-dairy whipped topping.

Trifle

To make this recipe you will need:
- One Basic White Cake (see page 137) baked, cooled and cut into small cubes
- Vanilla Pudding (see page 156) cooled
- 4 cups of Thickened Fruit (see page 39) of your choice
- 2 cups of non-dairy whipped topping or 2 cups of Pear Ice Cream (see page 158)

1. Layer the bottom of a glass serving bowl with about half of the cake cubes.
2. Spoon about half of the Vanilla Pudding over the cake cubes.
3. Spread 2 cups of Thickened Fruit over the pudding.
4. Layer the remaining cake cubes over the fruit and cover with the remaining Vanilla Pudding. Spoon final 2 cups of Thickened fruit over the pudding
5. Top everything with a whipped topping or Pear Ice Cream and serve immediately.

Serves 6 to 8

P

To prevent the cake pieces from getting too soggy, layer the trifle a few minutes before serving.

Vanilla Pudding

2	cups	water
1	cup	raw cashews, drained and rinsed
¼	cup	tofu milk powder
½	cup	honey
¼	tsp	vanilla or caramel flavoring
2	tsp	cornstarch
2	tsp	*Egg Replacer* or other commerical egg replacement product (optional)

pinch of salt

Makes 4 cups

1. Place all ingredients into blender and blend until smooth.
2. Pour mixture into a saucepan and cook over medium heat, stirring occasionally, until thick.
3. Remove from heat and allow to cool.
4. Pour into bowl or serving dishes and garnish with a sprinkle of cinnamon or mint leaf.

Tapioca Pudding

⅓ cup   minute tapioca
4   cups   water
1   cup   raw cashews
3   tbsp   soy milk powder
½   cup   honey
1   tsp   vanilla
1   tsp   maple flavouring
pinch of salt
1   cup   raisins (optional)

Makes 6 servings

1. Place tapioca in a small bowl. Add 1 cup of water. Microwave on high for two minutes. Stir. Continue microwaving until tapioca cooks or turns clear.
2. Place 1 cup water and cashews into blender and blend until smooth. Add 2 cups water, milk powder, honey, vanilla, maple flavouring and salt and blend again.
3. Pour blended mixture into a saucepan and, stirring constantly, bring to a slow boil.
4. Remove pot from stove and add cooked tapioca. Whisk mixture with a wire whip until well combined. Stir in raisins.
5. Pour pudding into serving dishes and chill overnight or until cold.

Raspberry Gelatin

3   cups   water
1   cup   frozen raspberry concentrate
1   cup   strawberry gelatin
1   tbsp   unflavored gelatin
2   cups   fresh or frozen fruit slices

Makes 6 servings

Try whipping the Raspberry Gelatin with a electric beater before serving to make it fluffier.

1. Boil water in a small saucepan.
2. Pour raspberry concentrate into a bowl, add gelatins, stir and let soak for 5 minutes.
3. Pour boiling water over gelatins and stir until gelatin is completely dissolved.
4. When slightly cooled, stir in fruit slices.
5. Pour into bowl or serving dishes and refrigerate until set.

Pear Ice Cream

1	cup	raw cashews
1	cup	pear juice (from canned pears)
¼	tsp	salt
1	tsp	vanilla
⅓	cup	honey or maple syrup
¼	cup	tofu drink mix (optional)
1		quart or 2, 14 oz tins canned pears

1. Place cashews and pear juice in blender and blend until creamy. Do not underblend.
2. Add remaining ingredients and blend well again.
3. Pour mixture into a flat 9" x 12" plastic container, cover and freeze.
4. When ready to serve, remove frozen mixture from freezer and cut it into 2" strips.
5. Put the frozen strips through a Champion Juicer and serve with your favorite desserts.

Serves 6

If you don't have a Champion Juicer, cut the frozen mixture into small cubes and puree them in a food processor or blender. Add a little tofu milk to help make it smooth. This recipe also works in a ice cream maker.

Pear Ice Cream Variations

Maple Walnut Ice Cream: Add 1 tablespoon of maple flavouring and ½ cup chopped walnuts or pecans to the basic recipe.

Fruit Sherbets: Replace pear juice with 1 cup of any flavor fruit juice concentrate (lime, orange, grape, etc.).

Fruit Ice Cream: Add 1 cup of your favorite whole fresh fruit (strawberries, raspberries, blueberries, sliced peaches, etc.) to the basic recipe.

Mocha Ice Cream: Add 1 cup carob chips and 2 tablespoons instant coffee substitute to the basic recipe.

Serves 6

Here are a few ice cream flavors you can make using the basic Pear Ice Cream recipe. Don't be afraid to experiment.

Alphabetical Index

Sectional Index

Silver Hills Bakery

At Silver Hills Guest House we promote a diet of fruits, nuts, grains and vegetables. We like to use grains and especially good breads at every meal. As the guest house grew from one room to its present size, we realized the need for a continuous supply of wholesome bakery products.

One of our staff members, Brad Brousson, decided he would like to start a bakery to meet the demand and supply our local community. Silver Hills Bakery was born in his mother's kitchen using her stove, countertop, table and telephone. With a lot of hard work, good recipes, and organic grain it has grown from its humble beginning into a bustling success. Silver Hills Bakery is supplying a variety of whole grain breads and granolas all over Western Canada. Everyone who samples their products becomes regular customers.

Silver Hills Guest House

The Silver Hills Guest House, established in 1985, is a lifestyle reconditioning center that offers a three-week, lifestyle program based on the eight natural remedies: exercise, water, fresh air, proper diet, sunlight, rest, abstemiousness and trust in Divine Power. Our Guest House is situated in the beautiful Mabel Lake Valley in southern British Columbia.

Some of our guests come for a health holiday and to experience the beauty of our endless nature trails. Others come because they enjoy the homey atmosphere and delicious vegetarian meals. Many of our guests suffer from a wide variety of what are commonly called the Western diseases: diabetes, obesity, heart disease, cancer and arthritis. Most of these health problems are the result of faulty lifestyle habits rather than physiological defects, and we have seen the dramatic and immediate improvements that result from forming simple, good health habits.

Because proper diet is one of the essential elements of good health, *The Best of Silver Hills* cookbook contains recipes for the vegetarian menus and foods we serve at the Silver Hills Guest House as part of our lifestyle reconditioning program. If you would like more information about our health program, tear out the request form and mail it to the address on it. We would be happy to hear from you.

Guest House

If you would like to receive more information about Silver Hills Guest House please clip out and send the following form to:

Silver Hills Guest House
R.R.#2, Site 10, Compartment 18
Lumby
British Columbia, Canada
V0E-2G0

Phone: (250) 547-9433
Fax: (250) 547-9488

E-Mail: shgh@junction.net
World Wide Web: http://www.tagnet.org/silverhills

Please send me more information about the lifestyle programs offered at Silver Hills Guest House

Name _____

Address _____

City _____

State/Province _____

Zip/Postal Code _____

Notes

Notes